Stanbrook Abbey

Gregorian Music

An Outline of Musical Palaeography

Stanbrook Abbey

Gregorian Music
An Outline of Musical Palaeography

ISBN/EAN: 9783743464902

Manufactured in Europe, USA, Canada, Australia, Japa

Cover: Foto ©Thomas Meinert / pixelio.de

Manufactured and distributed by brebook publishing software
(www.brebook.com)

Stanbrook Abbey

Gregorian Music

GREGORIAN MUSIC

AN OUTLINE

OF

MUSICAL PALÆOGRAPHY

ILLUSTRATED BY FAC-SIMILES OF ANCIENT MANUSCRIPTS

BY

THE BENEDICTINES OF STANBROOK

LONDON AND LEAMINGTON
ART AND BOOK COMPANY
NEW-YORK, BENZIGER BROTHERS
1897

TO

SAINT GREGORY AND SAINT AUGUSTINE

OUR APOSTLES

TO WHOM WE OWE THE FAITH AND THE SONGS

OF THE HOLY ROMAN CHURCH

THESE PAGES ARE DEDICATED

ON OCCASION OF THE THIRTEENTH CENTENARY

OF ENGLAND'S CONVERSION

PREFACE.

The following pages are an attempt to bring under the notice of English readers some results of recent researches in musical archæology. The subject is one of many-sided interest and offers to the musical specialist abundant matter for fascinating study. But we venture to think that this work will appeal to even the general reader, as giving, at least in outline, the main features of early Christian music, and of its development into what we know as Gregorian Chant.

We are mere gleaners, and have endeavoured to present only a *résumé* of the " Paléographie Musicale, " humble, it is true, yet sufficient, we hope, to convey a fair idea of the scope of that remarkable work. We have made use also of Dom J. Pothier's " Mélodies Grégoriennes, " a work which has opened up a vast field for the study of Plain-Chant, by placing it on a scientific basis.

We are glad to express our thanks to Dom A. Mocquereau, the able editor of the " Paléographie Musicale, " for much kind encouragement and assistance, and especially for putting at our disposal his two admirable papers, [1] from which we have drawn freely.

We are aware that the principles of Plain-Chant have recently been put forth in a very able publication of the Plain-Song and Mediæval Music So-

[1] " La Psalmodie Romaine & l'accent tonique latin. " — " L'art grégorien, son but, ses procédés, ses caractères. "

ciety. [1] The work is based, like ours, on the " Mélodies Grégoriennes " and the " Paléographie Musicale, " and it abounds with practical instructions which may be advantageously consulted by all Plain-Chant choirs. But, apart from the fact that its adaptation of English words to the ancient melodies is a *tour de force* scarcely likely to satisfy all critics, the " Elements of Plain-Song " does not profess to give the general *coup d'œil* of the *Paléographie* which has been our aim.

It is hoped that the perusal of the following pages may awaken an interest in the Church's Chant for its own sake — as an ecclesiastical art — even among those who are not called upon to co-operate in its practical restoration. The subject has, so far, received very little attention amongst us, and it is rare to meet with persons who take an intelligent interest in the matter. This lack of appreciation, to call it by a mild name, is no doubt largely due to the very faulty rendering of Plain-Chant, to which most of us are accustomed. But is it fair to condemn, merely on this evidence, an art hallowed by so many venerable associations, the chant of Canterbury, of Westminster, and of Sarum ! How fitting on the contrary that England, so conspicuous in the past for her love of the Liturgy, and still so true to the liturgical spirit, should be foremost in doing justice to that music which came to her with the faith, and which has been the delight of generations of her Saints and faithful children.

It was the Apostle of England, St. Gregory the Great, who organised and perfected the ecclesiastical chants, and the holy Pope, sending St. Augustine to his dear Angles, charged him to teach them the sacred songs of the Roman Church. Later on, St. Theodore, in his celebrated school at Canterbury, paid special attention to sacred music, and strove to spread its use ; for, up to that time, as Ven. Bede tells us, it was known only in Kent. At the same date, St. Benet Biscop's zeal had provided the Northern Monasteries with an illustrious master, in the person of Abbot John, Arch-Cantor of the Roman Church. St. Wilfrid, with his devotedness to Roman customs, was not likely to neglect the chant, and in fact we know that he introduced it wherever he

[1] " Elements of Plain-Song. " H. B. Briggs, London, 1895.

was able, chiefly by the help of two monks of Canterbury, one of whom was Eddi, the Saint's biographer.

The Synod of Clovesho, A.D. 747, showed great zeal for the preservation of the chant as received from Rome,[1] and prescribed its use in the whole Kingdom. To St. Dunstan we owe the well-known Kyrie " *Rex splendens,* " which he composed after hearing in ecstasy the songs of the Angelic choirs.

In later times we find several writers on Music, chiefly among the Monks, — Tunstede, for instance, and Walter de Odington, the latter a monk of Evesham and author of a remarkable work which presents a very complete account of the musical science of the 13th. century.

Emulating the example of our countrymen in all generations, let us show that we appreciate our treasures ; the songs of the primitive and mediæval Church are *ours,* they were inspired by the faith which we cherish, they were composed for a liturgical text which we still use, they are part of the glorious inheritance handed down to us by the Ages of Faith.

STANBROOK ABBEY.
Feast of St. Gregory the Great. 1896.

---

[1] " Ut uno eodemque modo dominicæ in carne sacrosanctæ festivitates in omnibus ad eas rite competentibus,... in cantilenæ modo celebrentur, juxta *exemplar quod scriptum de romana habemus Ecclesia.* Itemque ut per gyrum totius anni natalitia sanctorum uno eodemque die, juxta Martyrologium ejusdem romanæ Ecclesiæ, cum sua sibi convenienti psalmodia seu cantilena venerentur. '' (Councils and Ecclesiastical Documents. Haddan and Stubbs. Vol. iii. 367.)

TABLE OF CONTENTS.

		Page
CHAPTER I.	The Aim of Church Music .	1
CHAPTER II.	'' La Paléographie Musicale. ''	7
CHAPTER III.	The Origin of Neumatic Writing	13
CHAPTER IV.	Diastematic Notation .	19
CHAPTER V.	Liquescent Neums. .	28
CHAPTER VI.	Romanian Signs and Letters .	36
CHAPTER VII.	Rhythm .	45
CHAPTER VIII.	The '' Cursus. '' .	51
CHAPTER IX.	Adaptation of Texts	61
CHAPTER X.	Execution	70

APPENDIX.

Modes .	83
Psalmody .	86

PLATES. (See next page).

LIST OF PLATES.

1. Einsiedeln. MS. 121.

2. C. C. C. Cambridge. No. 473.

3. Montpellier. Bibl. de l'École de Médecine. No. 159.

4. Monza. Chapter. F. 3. 104.

5. Verona. Chapter. No. 105. F° 206.

6. Brit. Museum. Harl. 4951.

7. La Cava. (Choir-Gradual).

Plate 1.

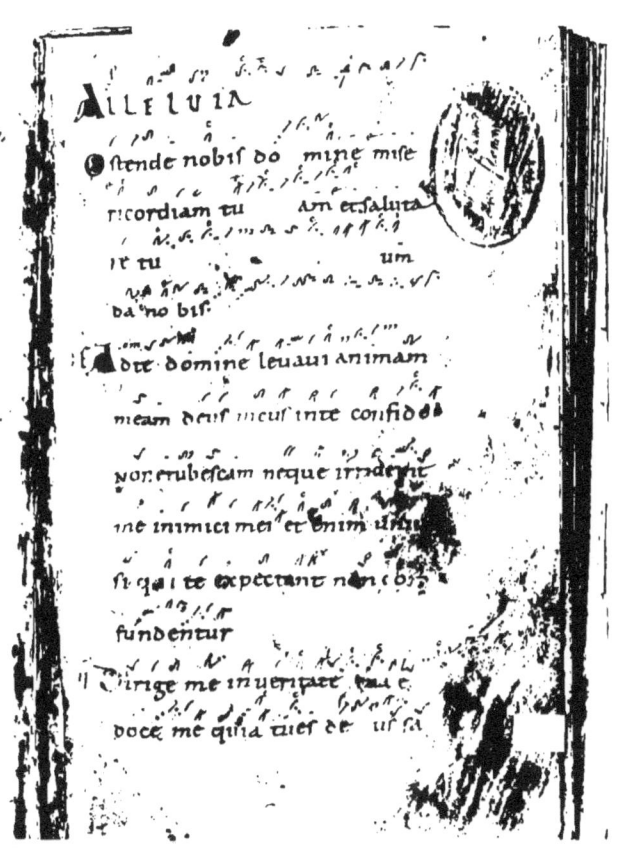

EINSIEDELN. MS. 121. ABBOT GREGORY'S GRADUAL. 10TH. CENTURY.
NEUM-ACCENTS, LIQUESCENT NEUMS, AND ROMANIAN SIGNS AND LETTERS.

Plate 2.

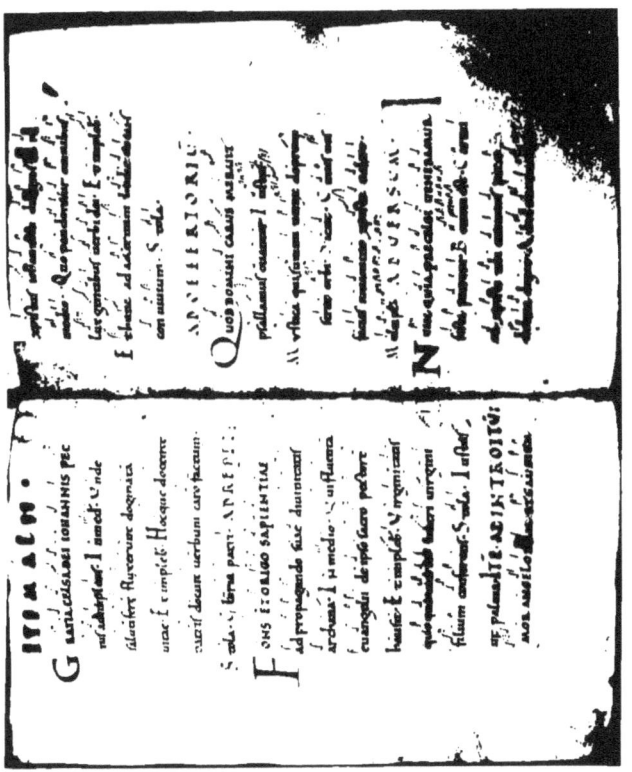

C. C. C. CAMBRIDGE. MS. 473. WINCHESTER TROPER. 11TH. CENTURY.
ANGLO-SAXON NEUM-ACCENTS.

Plate 3.

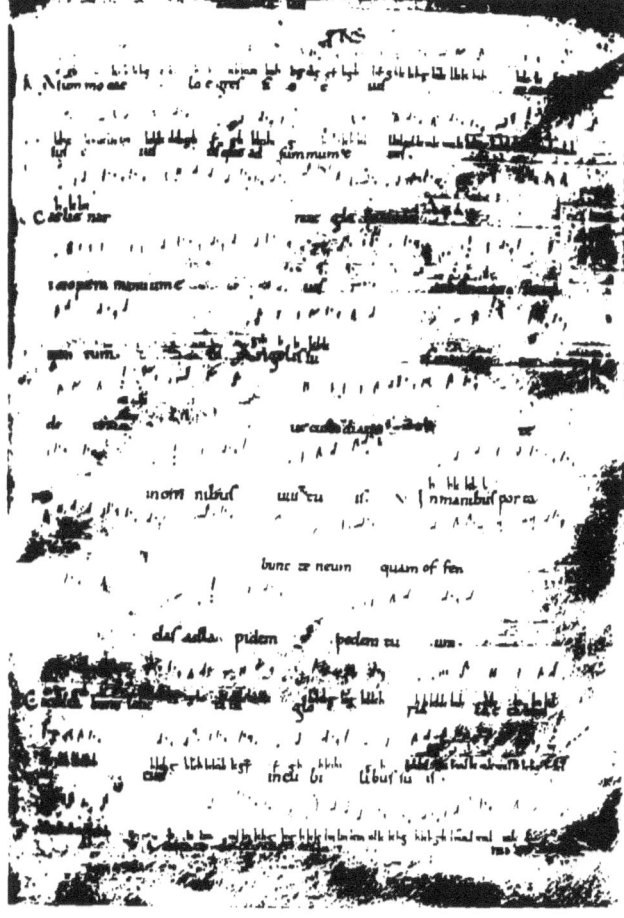

MONTPELLIER. MS. 11TH. CENTURY. BIBL. DE L'ÉCOLE DE MÉDECINE. 159.
TEXT IN RED. ALPHABETIC NOTATION AND FRENCH NEUM-ACCENTS.

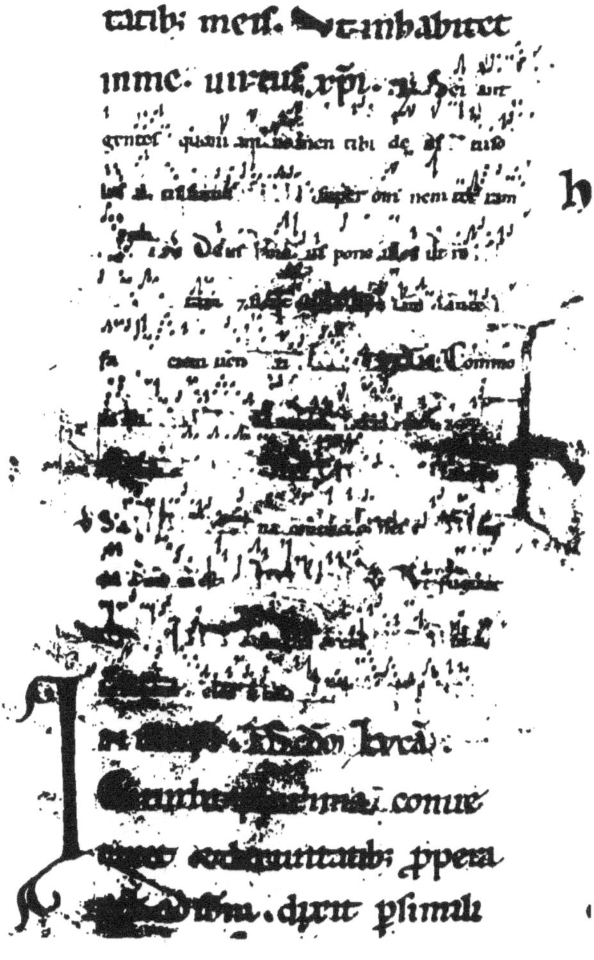

Plate 4.

MONZA. CHAPTER LIBRARY. F. 3, 104. 12TH. CENTURY GRADUAL.
ACCENTS AND POINTS MIXED.

Plate 5.

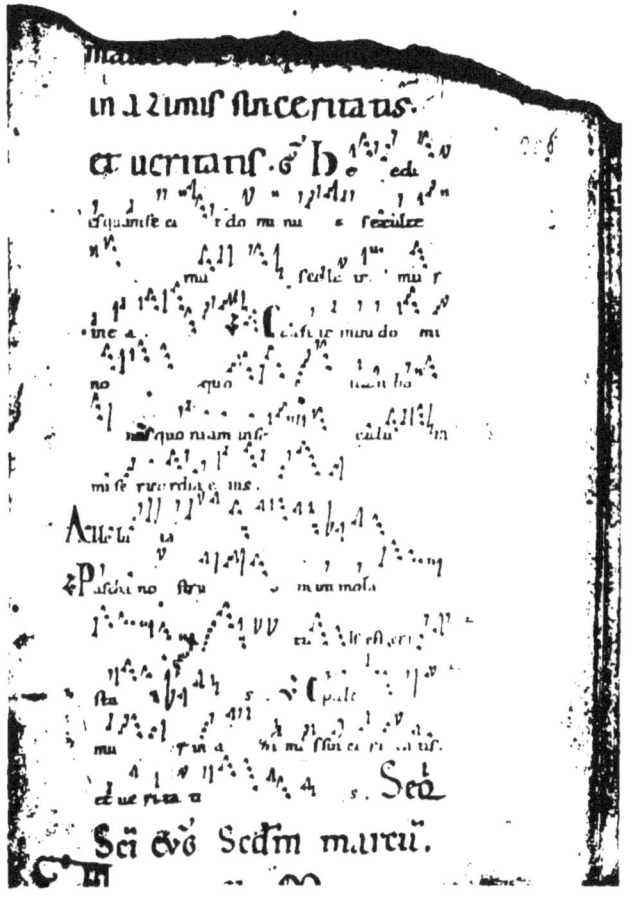

Plate 6.

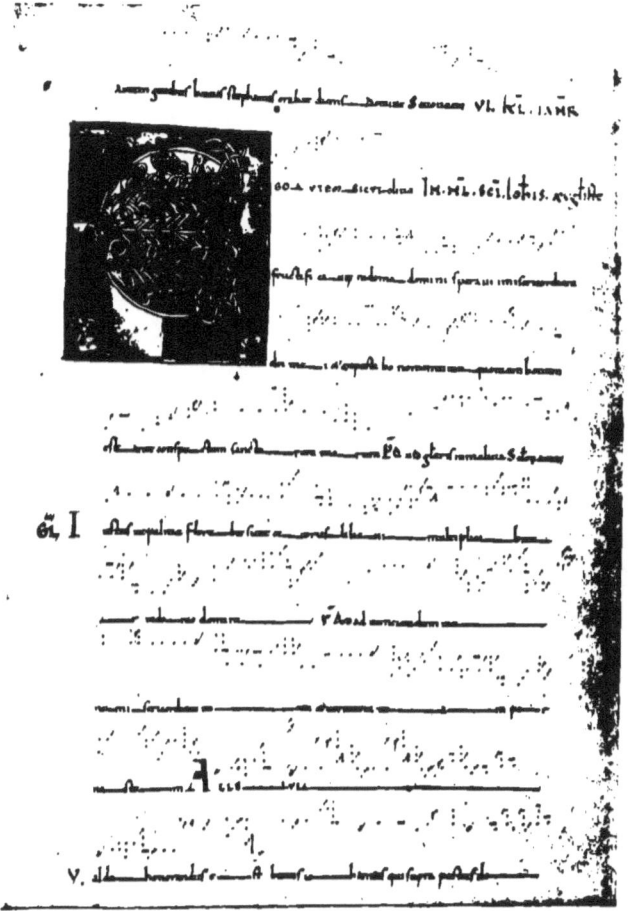

HARLEIAN MSS. Nº 4951. 11TH. CENTURY GRADUAL (FROM ST. STEPHEN'S, TOULOUSE).
AQUITANIAN NOTATION ON ONE DRY LINE.

Plate 7.

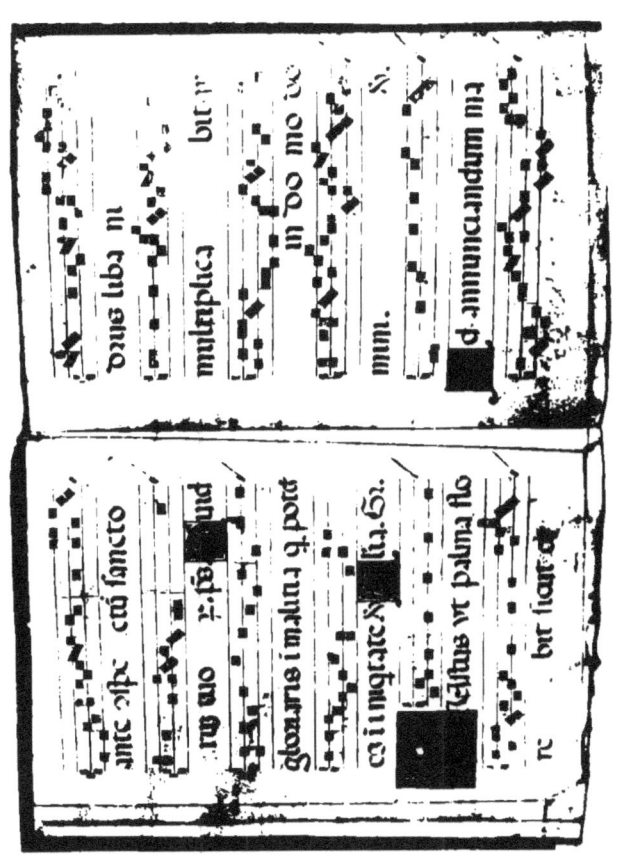

ABBEY OF LA CAVA. 15TH. CENTURY GRADUAL.

Plate 7.

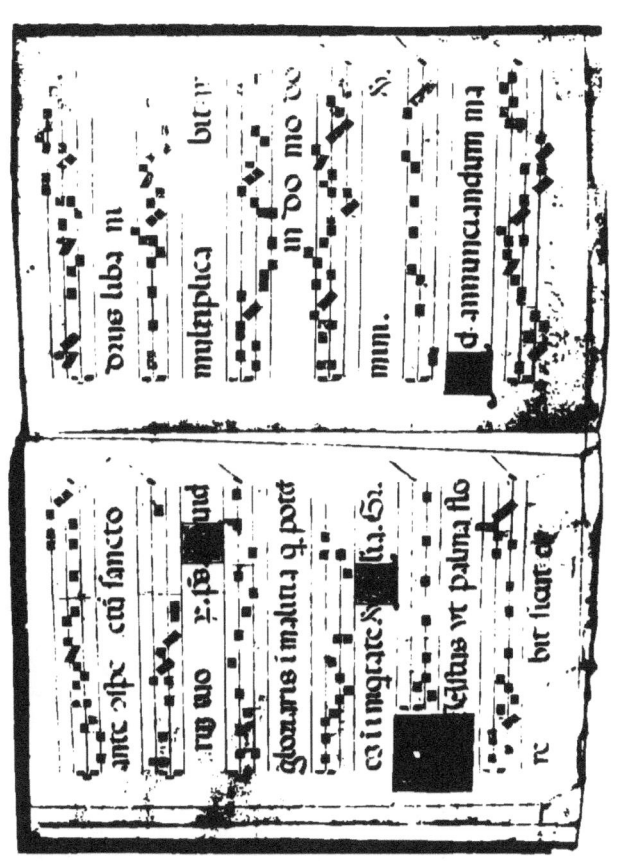

ABBEY OF LA CAVA. 15TH. CENTURY GRADUAL.

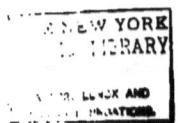

CHAPTER I.

THE AIM OF CHURCH MUSIC.

Music, I imagine, ought to end
in the love of the Beautiful.
(Plato, *Repub.* iii.)

" The movement of sound, so as to reach the soul for the education of it in virtue (we know not how), we call music. " Such was
Plato's ideal. Mr. Ruskin remarks on this passage that " the Greeks
only called *Music* the kind of sound which induced right moral feeling
(they knew not how, but they knew it *did*), and any other kind of
sound than that, however beautiful to the ear or scientific in composition, they did not call *Music* (exercise under the Muses), but *Amusia,*
— the denial or desolation for want of the Muses ".[1] The ancients
indeed considered music, not as a mere pastime, but as the necessary
basis of civilization and of all true education, and their youth were
brought under its influence that they might acquire from it a certain
balance and sweetness of character. Plato requires that the instructors
of youth " be able to choose out of imitative melody what is well and
ill-represented of the soul in its passion, and well discerning the picture

[1] " Fors Clavigera, " No. lxxxiii.

a

of the evil spirit from the picture of the good, they may cast away that which has in it the likeness of evil and bring forward that which has the likeness of good ; and hymn and sing that into the souls of the young, calling them forth to pursue the possession of virtue, by means of likenesses ''.[1]

These doctrines point to the great simplicity of all true art ; in such simplicity, such self-restraint, lies much of that marvellous power, which is able, by simple means, to produce the noblest results. By simplicity we do not mean that which characterises the expression of an art in its infancy, but simplicity in ideal, simplicity in choice of materials, simplicity in the manner of obtaining wonderful effects.

Holy Church, having appropriated all that was good, beautiful and true in the ancient world, became the depository of the arts, and enlisted their services in her cause. As to music, it became a constituent part of her worship. St. Paul had given the formal advice : " Teach and admonish one another in psalms, hymns and spiritual canticles, singing and making melody in your hearts to the Lord, " and the testimony of the earliest Christian writers shows that the precept was literally carried out.

But what will be the Christian ideal of music ? Will it be less noble than that of pagan antiquity ? May we not rather expect that the great truths of the Christian creed will inspire a still higher appreciation of the beauty of harmony ? Let us hear the Author of the " Ecclesiastical Hierarchy ", the sublime interpreter of sacred rites : " The sacred chants produce, in those who recite them in holy dispositions, an aptitude for either receiving or conferring the different Sacraments of the Church. The soul is prepared, by these sacred canticles, for the imme-

---

[1] Ruskin's translation, *loc. cit.*

diate celebration of the divine mysteries, and is brought into harmony with God, with her neighbour, and with herself ''.[1]

This conception of the funćtion of music is worthy of the Church and of the Divine Art. But where are we to find a musical system capable of realizing so lofty an ideal ? And firstly, can our modern music reach such heights ? It is not intended to renew here an oft-fought contest ; we think, however, that few will claim for the average Church-music of the day, that peaceful, elevating influence so commended in ancient chant both sacred and profane.

Of Palestrina nothing need now be said. His work has been often and ably treated, and the growing interest in his compositions is a happy sign. High, however, as is its charaćter, Palestrinian music is not the original song of the Church ; unless we agree that the honour of furnishing a form of chant worthy of celebrating divine mysteries and capable of raising the heart to God, was reserved for the sixteenth century.

What then of the earliest known music of the Roman Church ? Does *it* rise to the high ideal expressed above ? It is hoped that the following simple pages will give some answer to this question.

In this study, the *raison d'être* of religious music must ever be kept in view. The Church's life is centred in her Liturgy, — that wonderful cycle of prayer and praise. The text of this Liturgy, borrowed in great part from Sacred Scripture, is in itself sufficiently beautiful to dispense with all borrowed ornament. But the Church is not satisfied with merely *saying* her praise ; her loving enthusiasm urges her to song : '' La raison ne peut que parler, c'est l'amour qui chante ''.[2]

The Church sings too for another reason : knowing how much

---

[1] Migne, Gr. Patrol., Opp. S. Dion. Areop., *Eccles. Hier.*, iii.
[2] J. de Maistre.

the soul of man is influenced by all that strikes his senses, she appeals to music, the subtlest and most spiritual of the arts, as an auxiliary in the great work of human regeneration. " Music appeals primarily to the senses, but does not tarry within their bounds ; forcing a passage through them, it hurries onward to the soul, bearing on its strain the ' burden of the mystery ' of those facts of life and of living, which ' lie deeper down than any reasons that are to be found. ' " The great spiritual realities of life are indeed too deep, too far-reaching to be expressed in mere words. It has been beautifully said by the writer just quoted that while " Speech is but broken light on the depth of the unspoken, music is a mystical illumination of those depths, which the rays of language are too feeble to reach. While the achievement of language is to chisel into articulate permanence a clearly-defined thought, the mission of music is to give vent to such passions or *inspirations,* such imaginings or such *realities,* as are too subtle or too *mighty,* too dreamy or too *spiritual,* to be imprisoned within the thinkable terms of logic. Though necessarily less precise than speech, this is not by reason of the vagueness, but by reason of the vastness of its meaning, which thereby becomes proportionately overwhelming. While language is the crystallization of emotions from which the vital essence has escaped, and words, by defining, *limit,* — music is a revelation of the illimitable which lies behind all the barriers of time. " [1]

The Church then must sing. But whence will she derive her songs? Having been brought into touch with two civilizations and two forms of art, — the Hebrew and the Greco-Roman, — with exquisite tact she borrowed from each what best suited her ends. To the Hebrew Liturgy we owe the form of our psalmody ; the Church to this added

[1] Tablet, Feb. 16th. 1896. " *On the verbal music of Blank Verse.* "

her own songs and the first elements of these melodies she drew from Greco-Roman sources. The earliest Church chants, written in the diatonic form, were probably adapted, in at least a general way, to the scales and modes of the Greeks ; but there is no foundation for the statement of certain authors, that the very airs were borrowed from pagan songs.

Church music has not only its distinct aim ; it has also its proper characteristics. It is scarcely necessary to remark that this ancient art must not be judged by the rules of modern music. It is the growth of a civilization differing widely from ours ; its principles, unlike those of our music, are one with those of the classic melody of Greece and Rome. The beauties of such a system will never appear to a superficial observer, but any one who lays aside the prejudices of education and habit, and gives himself to the study, will be repaid by initiation into an exquisite art. To the musician, Plain-Chant is a revelation ; it leads him into a new sphere, where his ideas become enlarged and ennobled by the discovery of melodic riches undreamed of before.

Ancient Church music is all *song,* that is to say, it is always set to words. Here again we have the classic ideal ; music is the auxiliary of poetry, a development of speech, — or rather it *is* speech intensified to its fullest power. '' All perfectly rhythmic poetry is meant to be sung to music, and all entirely noble music to the illustration of noble words. '' — '' Songs without words '' would not indeed answer the end of sacred music. The Church's melody is not intended merely to suggest vague, pious thoughts or feelings, but to express deep theological truths, formal acts of faith, of hope, of love, and of praise.

Again, Plain-Chant is all in unison, hence it can have none of those dissonances on which modern music depends for many of its finest effects. On the contrary, it is ever simple and natural, and one would look in vain for sudden modulations, or in fact for any startling device. Herein lies much of the power and of the purifying influence of this music.

Gregorian *Tonality*, moreover, is totally unlike its modern name-sake, one of the most striking differences being that it has no *Leading-note*, that " joy for ever " to the modern musical ear. [1] When once the ear has become accustomed to the frank, clear Tonality of the Gregorian modes, it feels a certain distaste for the softer progressions of Chromatic intervals.

But perhaps absence of *Time* is the problem which most perplexes the modern musician in his study of Plain-Chant. Of this all-important question of Gregorian Rhythm, there will be more to say in a subsequent chapter.

These leading characteristics give to Plain-Song a certain dignity, a simplicity, a *convenance* (always supposing of course that the Chant is properly rendered), which produce that indescribable something which may be called unction. The influence it exercises on the heart of man is always elevating and purifying, and thus the Church finds this her song a powerful auxiliary in her mission of leading men to Him Who is infinite Beauty and Holiness.

The theme of this song is the vastest that may be ; it unites in one harmonious chorus the celebration of God's most mighty works and the yearnings and hopes of the human soul, blending both in a sweet hymn of adoration and thanksgiving.

[1] The subject of Tonality has been admirably handled in the *Elements of Plain-Song*, and the reader is referred to that work.

CHAPTER II.

" LA PALÉOGRAPHIE MUSICALE. "

It would be superfluous to call attention to the influence exerted on History and Archæology by the study of the first sources of those sciences. This method is not indeed the growth of our age, having produced many finished works as far back as the 16th. century; but its principles are now much more generally adopted, and, thanks to the production of fac-similes, almost every branch of Archæology is amply provided with collections reproducing its most ancient and reliable monuments.

Ecclesiastical music has shared, to some extent, in this movement. The attention of students once turned to the ancient notations, facsimiles of the MSS. followed almost necessarily. These publications, however, which date from the 17th. century, are not only few and far between, they are moreover short and inexact. In the present century there have been numerous reproductions of MSS. chants; but these, besides being imperfect representations of the originals, are, with the exception of a Gradual published by the Jesuit Père Lambillotte, too fragmentary to serve as foundation to any serious study of the ancient musical notations.

Since the appearance of Dom Pothier's " Mélodies Grégoriennes ",

(1880), the study of the *neums* (νεῦμα = a sign) [1] from being merely speculative has found its way into even the humblest methods of Plain-Chant. It is indeed impossible to teach the first principles of Gregorian music, without giving the pupil some idea of the origin, the nature, and the value of these neums. But students desirous of pursuing such studies have been hindered hitherto by the insufficiency of the published materials. To supply this want the learned Benedictines of Solesmes have undertaken the monumental work, which now enjoys an universal and well-earned reputation, " La Paléographie Musicale ". This publication, the fruit of much patient and persevering labour, includes the reproduction by phototypography of two entire Graduals (or, as they were formerly called, " Antiphonalia Missarum "), as well as of numerous specimens of notation ranging from the 9th. to the 17th. century and embracing all the countries of Europe. The soundness of the principles deduced from a conscientious and enlightened study of these MSS. is admitted by competent authorities, who do no hesitate to believe that we now possess, at least in great measure, the true rules for the interpretation, and, as we shall see, even for the practical rendering of the venerable Gregorian melodies. These rules, be it remembered, were lost — it was thought irretrievably lost — and have been reclaimed only at the cost of an indefatigable perseverance which is beyond all praise, and to which we are happy to pay here a humble tribute of admiration.

Let us then see what materials the musical archæologist has at his disposal, for the restoration of the Church's Chant, both in its form and in its execution. These materials are of three kinds, and are found

---

[1] *Neums* are certain *signs*, used in all ancient MSS. for the notation of ecclesiastical chant. These signs have nothing in common with the alphabetical characters of any language.

— 1st. In the works of the Fathers, Liturgists, and Latin Grammarians, as well as in the Chronicles of Churches and Monasteries ; — 2nd. In the musical treatises belonging to the Middle Ages ; — and 3rd. In the musical texts themselves, i. e. MSS. with musical notation.

The value of these three sources is by no means equal. With regard to the first class, it furnishes only indirect information on musical subjects. The documents of the second class are, it is true, more important ; yet, though their authors have undeniable intrinsic merit, they give us only here and there, and as it were by chance, those practical rules by which we set such store. There is nothing surprising in this when we remember the character of musical studies in the Middle Ages. Music was then rather a science than an art, being one of the branches of the Quadrivium, which, as is well known, consisted of Arithmetic, Music, Geometry, and Astronomy. To us this seems somewhat strange company for the divine art, and we naturally feel suspicious of theorists whose musical doctrines, borrowed from the Greeks and Romans, consist chiefly of speculations on the relation of sounds to numbers, or better still, on the harmony produced by the motions of the stars.[1]

Add to this peculiar view of Music the fact, that in the 9th. century (which is just the period at which such theorists as Aurelian, Hucbald, and the pseudo-Hucbald wrote), a methodical exposition of Gregorian chant was far from easy. The difficulty arose from the co-existence of two distinct elements : on the one hand, there was the Liturgical Music, which was already several centuries old, was connected

[1] No man, however proficient in execution, could be called a musician, unless thoroughly versed in this transcendental science. One text out of a thousand :
Musicorum & cantorum magna est distantia,
Isti dicunt, illi sciunt quæ componit musica :
Nam qui facit quod non sapit, diffinitur bestia.
(Musicæ Regulæ Guidonis. Cf. Gerbert Script.)

with classical times only by the general character of its tonality, and was preserved by tradition without any written theory. On the other hand, there were the principles of greco-roman music, which had survived the fall of pagan art, and which were still taught in the schools, at least theoretically. Here was a snare for our authors who failed to distinguish the two musical theories with sufficient clearness, and were inclined to apply the modal and rhythmical system of greco-roman art to ecclesiastical chant. Whatever useful information is gathered from these mediæval treatises, is the fruit of their authors' simple study of the liturgical melodies, without any admixture of greco-roman theories.

But, just when the science of Church Music was beginning to throw off the yoke of mathematics, a new difficulty arose in the increasing influence of Time and Harmony. Up to the 10th. century, these elements had been merely popular and practical, but from that time they aimed at obtaining a place in the schools of chant. The theoretical writers of the time, carried away by this new current, turned their attention to the mysteries of Time and of counterpoint, to the almost total neglect of Church Music. Henceforth there are two distinct kinds of music, plain or unmeasured (*immensurabilis*), and measured (*mensurabilis*) music, — and consequently, two distinct theories.

It is therefore evident, that in studying the musical treatises bequeathed to us by the Middle Ages, we must be careful to distinguish three currents : viz. greco-roman doctrine, Gregorian principles, and the rules of the Mensuralists.

To come now to the third class of monuments, the Texts of the music itself. These documents are, beyond comparison, the most reliable foundations for the study of sacred chant. In them we find all the desired information regarding the version, the rhythm, the tonality, and the notation of ecclesiastical music. True, they furnish no formal principles ; but they are the substantial expression of both theory and practice, they are the translation into writing of the teaching and of the execution of the old masters. Hence their importance, and their superiority to theoretical treatises.

Fifty years ago the neums of these MSS. were a closed letter. Many systems of interpretation have since been ventilated, but these, though containing some true principles, have proved to be, on the whole, in contradiction with the MSS. themselves and with history. Patient study has however overcome all obstacles, and it is now universally acknowledged that these neums may be read and analysed, and, (if we may use the expression) translated, by the help of three distinct classes of documents, in which the melody is represented either by (1) points written one above another, or by (2) letters of the Alphabet, or lastly, by notes written on lines.

The Chant of the Western Church alone offers a wide field for interesting study, but we shall here confine ourselves to the songs of the Church of Rome. We may however notice in passing that the chants known as Ambrosian, Gallican and Mozarabic are in their chief features identical with the Roman, from which indeed they seem to be derived, so that the four classes may be likened to so many dialects of one and the same language. The notation, too, is the same in all, i. e. neumatic writing, characterised of course by the peculiarities of each country's caligraphy.

Let us then, taking advantage of the labour of previous students, learn some of the precious secrets hidden in the dusty parchments of neumatic MSS. We shall gain from the study a deeper and more reasonable appreciation of the songs of our Mother, the Holy Roman Church, — songs to which their association with St. Gregory the Great adds fresh interest. For it was he whose master-hand brought into unity, developed and enriched the already-existing Church Music, and who bequeathed to us among the many blessings of his fruitful Pontificate, a collection of sacred chants, the fruit of a civilisation which had its roots in the classic age, and which availed itself of the happiest inventions of human genius for the adornment of the Divine Truths of Christianity.

CHAPTER III.

ON THE ORIGIN OF NEUMATIC WRITING.

Let us for the moment lay aside whatever knowledge we may have of modern music, with its inseparable associates, Staves, Leger lines, Clefs, Keys, etc., etc., and let us try to trace the notation of Liturgical Chant from its beginning. The subject is not without interest to even the modern musician, since the system of notation with which he is familiar is the outcome of the Roman Church's earliest attempts at music-writing.

The connection between speech and chant is obvious, the essential difference being that in speech the modulations of the voice are undetermined, whilst in chant the melody advances by fixed intervals, which the ear can assign to a definite position in the scale of sounds. It is therefore not surprising to find the primitive signs of a musical notation in the accents which regulate the inflexions of the voice in speaking. These accents (acute, grave, circumflex and anticircumflex) from which all the *neumatic* and *modern* systems of notation are derived, are figures originating naturally in oratorical modulations of voice, and as we shall see, wonderfully fitted for their purpose.

It is plain that sounds, by their very nature, are incapable of representation : " Soni, nisi memoria retineantur, pereunt. "[1] If they are to be preserved, it must be by means of some expressive symbol. In

[1] S. Isid., *Etymol.*, iii, 15.

the case of oratorical notation, such a symbol was soon found, being
borrowed from the gesture of the speaker. We know how intimate is
the conne&ion between voice and hand ; both are ruled simultaneously
by movements of the soul : " Gestus & ipse voci consentit, & animo
cum eo simul paret. "[1] So true is this and so natural, that the very
accents are merely graphic representations of those gestures, and take
their form from the motion of the speaker's hand. Quintilian's descrip-
tion of gestures applies with equal fitness to accents : " Optime autem
manus a sinistra incipit, " — is not this the *acute* accent (/) traced
upward from left to right ? " In dextra parte deponitur " — here is the
grave accent, also drawn from left to right, but downward (\ ).

Let us now follow these accents in their application to diatonic
melodies. With regard to the *acute* accent, (Virga), we find it entire in
the six groups or neums which are the foundation of all the rest, and
we notice that, whether alone or in composition, it invariably denotes
an *elevation* of voice.[2]

In the	*Clivis,*	first stroke	∧	
	Podatus,	second stroke	⌐	
	Torculus,	middle stroke	∫	
	Porre&us,	1st. and 3rd. strokes	⋏	
	Scandicus,	highest note	⌐/	
	Climacus,	first note	/∴	

The grave accent preserves its normal shape in the *Clivis* (2nd.
stroke) and *Porre&us* (middle stroke) — but becomes slightly altered
in the other groups, being either made horizontally or reduced to a mere
point — hence its name " *Pun&um* ". The inverse of the Virga or acute
accent, the Pun&um or grave accent always represents a fall of the
voice.

[1] Quintil., *Inst. Orat.*, xi, 3.   [2] See Plates 1 et 2.

The Circumflex and Anticircumflex, which practically are mere combinations of the acute and grave accents, figure respectively in the Clivis and Podatus.

The chief features of this Chironomic Notation (Χείρ = hand, νόμος = rule) — in its application to both oratory and music, may be summed up as follows :

(1) The respective *position* of the accents is of no consequence; the musical value, the pitch of a note, depends on the direction in which the sign is traced. Thus, the acute accent invariably marks an elevation of voice, whether it be written higher or lower in any given series of accents. (2) From this it follows that it is the *whole* sign which expresses the note, not the beginning nor the end of the stroke. (3) The accents indicate an *indefinite* rise or fall, as the case may be. (4) The accents have no value as expressions of time or force.

These then are the forms of notation in Liturgical music. But how did they give the melody, the *air* as we should say? To understand this we must go back to the period when the oratorical accents were transferred to the domain of music, for it is clear that this primitive notation would not have been originally suited to express the elaborate compositions of later ages. The very use of such signs, for notation, presupposes extreme simplicity in the chants of the early Roman Church, and as a matter of fact, nothing could be simpler than those melodies which were nearly allied to the natural modulations of speech. Such pieces being easily learned and remembered, the oratorical accents were considered quite sufficient to express them. It must not be forgotten that the only notation available at that time was the alphabetic system of the Greeks, and this was unnecessarily complicated for application to such simple types.

As the Chants developed, the neum-accents easily lent themselves to the growth, and groups of four, five or more notes were formed by combining the simple neums given above.

TABLE OF THE PRINCIPAL NEUMS.

	NAME.	FORM.	ELEMENTS.	MODERN NOTES.
1	Punctum	· -	*Grave acc.* (g.)	
2	Virga	/	*Acute acc.* (a.)	
3	Pes or Podatus	⌡	g. a.	
4	Clivis	⋀	a. g.	
5	Scandicus	⸴/	g. g. a.	
6	Climacus	/·.	a. g. g.	
7	Torculus	⋀	g. a. g.	
8	Porrectus	N	a. g. a.	
9	Porrectus flexus	M	a. g. a. g.	
10	Scandicus flexus	⸴⋀	g. g. a. g.	

NAME.	FORM.	ELEMENTS.	MODERN NOTES.
11. Torculus resupinus	_N_	g. a. g. a.	
12. Climacus resupinus	/·./	a. g. g. a.	
13. Pes subbipunctis	J·.	g. a. g. g.	

But how did these groups express the various intervals of the scale? How could one tell, e. g. what distance was marked by a Poda-tus (√) or Clivis (∧), since the neum might represent, according to the ancients, any one of thirteen intervals? The enigma may be solved by considering a parallel example in speech. In English, the word *ward* has six meanings. Yet, meeting it in reading, we see at a glance what it means, because we know our language and are quite sure that in such a context the word has such a meaning. This is exactly the process by which the neum-accents were interpreted; the Cantor knew his melo-dies by heart, an indispensable qualification, and he saw at a glance that a Podatus for instance in such a connection must represent such an interval. We are not prepared to maintain that the system was re-markable for its simplicity, for indeed it severely taxed the memory of the poor Cantor [1]. The realisation of its difficulties prepares us for the

[1] ·· Mirabiles autem cantores & cantorum discipuli, etiamsi per centum annos cantent, numquam per se sine magistro unam vel saltem parvulam antiphonam canta-bunt; tantum tempus in cantando perdentes, in quanto & divinam & saecularem scri-pturam potuissent plene cognoscere. '' (Guido Aretinus, *De ignoto cantu*.)

'' Sed cantus adhuc per hæc signa (i. e. neumata) minus perfecta cognoscitur, nec per se quisquam eum potest addiscere, sed oportet ut aliunde audiatur & longo usu dis-catur, & propter hoc hujus cantus nomen *usus* accepit. '' (Joan. de Muris, *Summa Mu-sicæ*, cap. vi.)

c

otherwise astonishing fact — that ten years was the modicum of training required for a singer, who was absolutely obliged to possess all the Liturgical chants " in theca cordis. "

As a matter of fact, then, the neum-accents served, especially in elaborate pieces, merely as guides and reminders, showing clearly the *number* of notes to be sung and the manner of *grouping* them, but indicating only indefinitely a rise or fall of pitch. [1]

The insufficiency of this notation must have been felt early, for from the 9th. century we find attempts at reform, and the beginnings of a new and really *musical* system, in which the notes are written on a graduated scale according to the respective distances of the musical intervals.

The transition to this new system affords matter for interesting study and will be the subject of the next chapter.

[1] See Plate 1.

CHAPTER IV.

DIASTEMATIC NOTATION.

We saw in the last chapter how the oratorical accents came to be adopted as signs of musical notation, and we hinted at the insufficiency of a system which indicated only indefinitely the intervals of sound. We are thus prepared to find masters seeking some means of supplying the deficiencies of their notation.

One of the first attempts in this direction was the use of the letters of the Alphabet to express the different notes. These letters were generally used with the neum-accents, to which they were added by way of translation. We are told that St. Odo of Cluny noted a complete Antiphonary in this way. His work has unfortunately perished, but we have a complete Codex (Montpellier MS.) [1] as well as various fragments of this notation. From these it seems that the system was intended almost exclusively for teaching purposes. At least it was never widely used in liturgical books, for by its side there was forming a new kind of notation, which aimed at showing the pitch of notes by writing the neums either higher or lower according to their position in the scale of sounds.

Since " The human mind seems to have an innate tendency to represent sounds as if contained in a vertical straight line ", (M. Gevaert.) one might suppose that some graphic system corresponding to

[1] See Plate 3.

this idea would early have been invented. Yet centuries passed before anything of the kind was attempted. The Greeks with their Alphabetic notation seem never to have dreamed of such a thing; oratorical accents gave no idea of the various intervals, and perhaps Diastematic (διάστημα = interval) notation would never have been invented, had not the neum-accents existed as the materials out of which a perfect representation of the musical scale has been produced.

Yet, Diastematic notation differs widely from Chironomic. In the latter, as we have seen, a rise or fall of pitch is expressed by the *form* of the sign, by the direction in which the sign is traced; for instance, the *acute* accent (/) always marks a rise. In the former, the musical value of a sign depends on its *position* on the staff.

The first signs of the new system appear about the 9th. century. in the neum-*points* gradually spaced according to intervals, long even before the invention of lines. This is already a great advance from the neum-accents written over the text, either high or low, without other rule it seems than the copyist's caprice. For the origin of these neum-points, we must look to the neumatic accents of which they are the natural development and the perfection.

It will perhaps be well to give at once a Table showing the progressive transformations of the neum-accents.

NEUM-ACCENT.
ALTERATIONS.
MODERN NOTES.
Virga
Clivis
Porrectus
Podatus
Torculus
Climacus

The changes visible in each group are due primarily to the inclina-
tion of writers to facilitate their work by giving the neums a more
cursive form. Copyists of all ages have been ingenious in finding expe-
dients for saving time and trouble. In the musical scribe this instinct
first shows itself in a tendency to shorten the strokes of the neum-
accents ; points next appear at the extremities of the accents, whilst the
accents often disappear completely and give place to points.

It seems that these transformations of the neums first suggested
the idea of spacing the notes according to intervals ; at first the *groups*
are spaced, then the *notes* of each group begin to be written according
to the desired intervals. These first attempts were not to be unproduc-
tive. At first, the intervals were shown, more or less, but they still
remained rather indefinite, and the transcription of the notes thus spaced
called for a scrupulously careful copyist. [1] But now a bright idea
occurs to some anxious scribe : why not utilise the blind line drawn
for the text and make it the starting point of the notation ? Why not,
for instance, call the line *Fa* and thus give some guide for the rest of
the notes ? Here we have notation on *one* line, which may be seen in
many MSS. [2]

The method is a vast improvement, but it does not remove all
difficulties, for the further the notes are from this line, the more doubtful their pitch becomes. This suggests a second line, representing *Ut* :

[1] See Plate 5.
[2] See Plate 6.

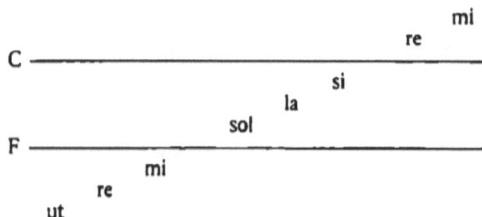

Having got so far, additional lines were soon adopted, until the staff of *four* was found to be sufficient.

The invention of this system is commonly ascribed to Guy of Arezzo, but a study of the MSS. proves that the method, which had been forming for two centuries before his time, is the work of the theorists and copyists of those ages. What Guy did was to perfect the system by fixing the Clefs and the *number* of lines. It is important to bear this in mind, as the fact is one of the strongest guarantees for the authenticity of the Gregorian melodies. Had the chants been translated by Guy or any other individual into a notation entirely of his own invention, the tradition would be open to doubt, as we should have no assurance that he had always interpreted the neums aright. But when we find that " the transition from neums without lines to diastematic neums has come slowly, progressively, simultaneously in all parts of Europe, and by means which vary with MSS. and places, — circumstances which prove that the neumists in their attempts at improving notation worked independently of one another, — we have every reason to believe in the identity of the melodies, whether noted chironomically or diastematically. " [1]

The introduction of lines had considerable influence on the form

[1] *Pal. Mus.*, t. ii, p. 160.

of the neums, by requiring them to be written very exactly on the desired degree of the staff. A Virga (/), for example, placed on lines would be almost as vague as if written in *campo aperto*.

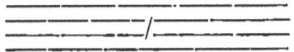

In this case the note might be either on the first or second space, or on the second or the third line. To remove all ambiguity the copyist adds a *point* representing the note :

By this means the point becomes the essential part of the sign, and the accent remaining as a relic of the original neum serves as a connecting line for the notes of each group, which thus preserves almost its primitive form. (See Table, p. 20.) — As to those groups in which the notes are sometimes *diamonds*, sometimes *squares*, sometimes again *points*, these peculiarities are merely material, depending solely on the shape of each writer's pen and on his manner of handling it.

Side by side with the *Neum-points,* in which the original accents are preserved as ligatures, we have another class of neumatic figures, i. e. *Detached-points.* We saw an indication of this system even in Chironomic notation, where the grave accents of Climacus and Scandicus were replaced by mere points, on account of the inconvenience of making several consecutive accents in the same direction. Thus Climacus ⌢ became /·, Scandicus ⌡ became /. The same process was soon applied to other neumatic groups.[1] Some copyists set to work boldly and transform all the neums past recognition. Others proceeding more timidly change only a few of the signs, and thus we sometimes finp

[1] See Plate 4.

both *detached* and *connected* points in the same MS. A glance at the
following Table will satisfy us that these detached points are derived,
like *neum-points,* from the primitive neum-accents.

NAME.	NEUM-ACCT.	TRANSITION.	DETACHED-POINTS.
Climacus	⌐ /:	⌐ /:	⫶
Scandicus	⌡ /	⌡ /	⌐ ⫶
Podatus	⌡	/	⌐ ⫶
Torculus	⌠	⌐	⌐ ⌐
Clivis	⋀	⌐	: ⌐
Porrectus	*N*	⋁	⫶ :⌐

The system of detached-points prevailed in nearly the whole of
Spain and in Aquitaine, and became quite a distinct kind of notation. [1]
In other parts it seems to have been fused with the system of connected-
points, so that both forms of notation arrive at the same result by
different means. In the connected-points, points are added to the accents;
while in the detached-points, accents are added to the points.

      Connected-points.   *Detached-points.*

    ⌒   became ⌒   ⋰ became ⌒

In both systems we remark the care of copyists to preserve the
traditional manner of *grouping* the notes, which is an essential point.
A Porrectus, e. g. may assume a dozen different shapes, but it remains
a Porrectus still, a group, that is, of three notes *N* (acute, grave, acute).
It is to be regretted that our modern chant books, completely ignoring
or at least disregarding this important point, reduce the succession of
groups, each with its own accent and character, to an incoherent string

[1] See Plate 6.

of notes, which '' drag their slow length along '' in unrelieved heaviness. [1]

Compare the following :

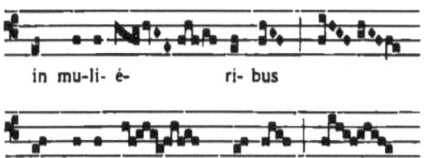

in mu-li- é-   ri- bus

May we be allowed a word on the practical bearing of some of the facts mentioned in this paper? Firstly with regard to the Virga, known as the *tailed* and therefore (why *therefore?*) the long note.

We have seen that in the system of neum-accents it originally consisted of a tail only (/) and that its head was added to specify the note; whilst in the neum-point system, by the irony of fate, it consisted of only a head and became possessed of a tail by evolution. So much for facts. After the introduction of the staff, the *virga* had no longer the same *raison d'être* as before (the notes being then determined not by the form of the sign, but by its position on the staff), and it became a mere matter of choice whether a Virga or a Punctum (i. e. a tailed note or a square) should be used for a single note. In most MSS. the Virga is employed arbitrarily, but in some it is pretty regularly used for the first syllable of each word, in others for the last, while in others it is invariably employed for every note standing alone. It is plain then that to the minds of those who used the Virga in such varied ways, the tailed note had no value as to time.

Another proof of this fact is found in a very interesting MS. of

[1] See Plate 7, where the groups are preserved.

d

the 11th. century [1]. The last page of this volume gives several Alleluiatic
verses, noted with a double line of neums, or, as we should say, in
two parts. The ordinary melody is written immediately over the text,
and the second part over that. The second voice corresponds, note for
note, to the first, and generally proceeds by contrary motion. Now in
these two parts a *punctum* in one voice corresponds to a *Virga* in the
other — a *clivis* to *podatus*, *torculus* to *porrectus*, *scandicus* to *climacus*.
If the Virga be a long note, the corresponding groups must be translated thus :

This is obviously impracticable and we are forced to believe that
a virga or a punctum has of itself no value as an expression of time.

The same is to be said of diamond notes. Their form is due simply
to their being made with a broad pen held obliquely.

How surprised the good old Monastic scribes would be, could
they hear the theories evolved from the accidental squares, tails, or
diamonds traced by their unwitting pens. They would learn the importance of a tailed note, the respectable mediocrity of a square, and the
insignificance of a diamond. No doubt their first practical lesson would
be that in singing for instance a Climacus they should duly hold
on the tailed note and dispatch the diamonds with the least possible
delay.

We do not, however, mean to say that in Plain Chant all the notes
are of absolutely equal length, for this is far from the truth. The principle which we would insist on is this — that one must not seek

---

[1] Biblioth. de la Ville de Chartres, No. 130.

indications of the time-value of a note in its *shape*, for this value depends, not on the shape of the note, but, if we may say so, on circumstances, and chiefly on the words to which the music is set. This is especially the case with syllabic chant, for then each note has simply the value of the syllable which it accompanies, the accent of each word being well marked, and the weak syllables sung softly, but not hurriedly. As a matter of fact, it is more a question of *loud* and *soft,* than of *long* and *short.* It is unnecessary to remark that a pause must be prepared for by a *ritardando* in the notes which precede it.

In more elaborate pieces the value of notes is fixed by several rules. We shall see farther on that the Romanian Letters and Signs are freely used to mark the relative duration of sounds. The *position* too of a note will often determine its time-value.

We here mention these few facts, lest what we have previously said should lead to the conclusion that the Church's Chant is devoid of artistic feeling, which would assuredly be the case, did it require an absolutely equal value for every sound.

CHAPTER V.

LIQUESCENT or SEMIVOCAL NEUMS.

Having now made acquaintance with the neums in their primitive form, and having sketched their subsequent history, let us return to the early MSS., and try to get some insight into the art of the Gregorian melodies.

The neum-accents are derived, as we have seen, from the accents used in oratory; this fact gives us the first hint of the close connection which exists between text and melody in these venerable compositions. This connection will be made more evident the farther we advance in our study, for we shall see how words and music are fused, and how in fact the melody is simply a development of the accent of the text.

We purpose to consider now certain details of notation, which prove plainly the influence of the words on the music, and show how exactly the liturgical musicians appreciated the fusion of these two elements, and how ingeniously they represented this fusion in their notation.

" In singing, and indeed in reading also, the passage from one syllable to another requires special attention; at the moment of such transition the singer or reader must be most vigilant, so that, amidst the evolutions of the voice, he may ensure a harmonious flow of the syllables, and preserve not only the unity of the word, but the finish and completeness of the smallest details of pronunciation. These conditions are essential to the flow of the rhythm and the clearness of the text. "[1] For this end, Gregorian composers and Cantors employed various means, all which show that the liturgical music, in its best days, was composed and rendered with consummate art and true esthetic sense. We will confine ourselves here to one of these methods, the use of Liquescent or Semivocal Neums.

Musical Liquescence is thus defined by Guy of Arezzo : " Liquescunt in multis voces, more litterarum, ita ut inceptus modus unius ad alterum limpide transiens nec finiri videatur. " Which may be thus paraphrased : " As in the Alphabet there are *liquids* (l, m, n, r,), so there are liquid *sounds*. These occur at the passage from one syllable to another, when a note which began full and entire expires, as it were, and is fused with the next note. "

Liquescence is in fact a delicate shade of pronunciation reflected in the melody and consequently marked in neumatic notation. This half-sounded (semivocalis) note which thus dies away (liquescit, deficit) at the transition to a new syllable, is consequent on certain combinations of consonants or of vowels. Before entering on the study of these combinations, an introductory remark will not be out of place.

Musical Liquescence originated at a time when Latin was pronounced with all the purity and correctness of a living language, and it may be illustrated by a similar fact in grammar. In Greek and in Latin a short vowel becomes long by position before two consonants. The cause of this seems to be the difficulty which the ancients had in pronouncing several consonants consecutively. To a short vowel of

---

[1] *Paléog. Musicale*, t. ii.

one beat they added a pause equal to a fraction of another beat. This pause is defined as " a momentary interruption between two consonants, in pronouncing the syllables of a word. "[1] Yet this interruption is not a silence; it consists rather in the insertion of an indistinct vowel, an *arrière-son*, which is not part of the preceding consonant, but which results from the suspension of the effort required for pronouncing that consonant. "[2] This may be seen by pronouncing quickly and distinctly a word like *sub^e-dat^e*. The exact articulation of each group of syllables explains the kind of resonance which seems to separate them, v. g., *con^e-fun^e-dan^e-tur. sal^e-ve*.

Now this grammatical principle applies exactly to semi-vocalisation; it is precisely this *arrière-son*, this delicate shade of pronunciation, that influences the melody and even the material form of the neums. This half-vowel used, through ignorance, to be written in many words; in MSS. and inscriptions of all ages such examples as the following frequently appear : Pet(e)ro, uber(i)tas, aug(i)mentum, ur(e)bem, and it is just in such words that liquescent or semivocal notes are found. In words, this insertion is a blemish, because a full vowel is added; in chant, it is an ornament, introducing only a feeble note, naturally called for by an exact pronunciation. In practice, Liquescence may be likened to *portamento di voce*, which, when judiciously employed, adds so much to a melody.

We may now notice the principles which regulate the use of semivocal notes :

I. Liquescents are never found in the course of a vocalise, a fact which proves that they result from the influence of the text.

II. Every Liquescent comes at the *end* of a group and serves as

[1] M. Edon. " Écriture & prononciation du latin savant & du latin populaire, " p. 213.
[2] *Paléog. Mus.*, t. ii, p. 43.

transition to a new *syllable*. This does not however imply that the
final of every group before a new syllable is liquescent; because,

III. In order to produce semivocalisation the notes must be in contact with syllables the letters of which call for such treatment.

IV. Paradoxical as it may seem, semivocal sounds are not *always*
employed when such combinations of letters occur.

Let us examine these facts more closely. I and II require no com-
ment, but we must pause at III. We have said that in order to produce
Liquescence, the notes must be in contact with syllables the letters of
which call for such treatment. The phonetic concurrences which require
Liquescence are mainly : — 1st. At the meeting of two consonants,
the first of which is a liquid, v. g. *palma, super cælos, tempus, scientia*.
This is the commonest kind of Liquescence. The musical effect may be
seen in the following example :

The notes susceptible of Liquescence here are the last note of the Clivis
(col. 1.) and the last of the Podatus (col. 2.); but with the word *ædi-
ficavit* there is no call for semivocalisation. Sing to the same notes
the word *inventus* :

Here the *sol* of the Clivis and the *ut* of the Podatus have become
liquescent, because of their contact with the letter *n*, the exact pronun-

ciation of which calls for a kind of half-vowel. The semivocal notes
might be thus translated :

Non   est   in- ᵉ-   ve- nᵉ-   tus

— 2nd. At the meeting of two consonants, the first of which is a den-
tal (t, d) : v. g. u*t* *d*iscam, a*d* *t*e. These letters produce Liquescence
only when they come at the end of a word, for it is only then that they
have a resonance. (Cf. *ta* and *at*). — 3rd. At the meeting of two consonants, the first of which is *s :* " sacer*dos* magnus ". — 4th. When the
consonants *gn* come together in the body of a word : " magnus ". —
5th. When certain consonants (d, m, n, r, t, b, s, l), are followed by *j*.
— 6th. Semivocal notes are very frequently used with the diphthong
au " autem ". — 7th. There are also examples of Liquescence caused
by single consonants, for instance *m* and *g :* " se*m*itas, re*g*i. "

Other instances are so rare that they are mere exceptions.

IV. We have yet to examine our last principle. It seems very
contradictory to state that, in spite of the truth of what has been said
above, semivocal sounds are not always employed when such combinations of letters occur. We must bear in mind that in Liquescence there
are two things to consider, viz. text and melody. The text must con-
tain letters susceptible of Liquescence and the rhythm and melody must
be in a condition to allow of its application. As a rule the music easily
lends itself to the requirements and even to the caprices of the words,
yet *as* music it has inalienable rights, which it cannot sacrifice without
endangering the harmony of its parts. The result of Liquescence is to
make the sounds which it affects almost imperceptible, semivocal, and
therefore it cannot be admitted in certain notes the fulness of which

is essential to the purity and perfection of the musical phrase. Moreover, liquescence sometimes takes the form of an additional note, and in many instances such an addition would injure both the rhythm and melody.

NOTATION OF LIQUESCENTS. (1st. CLASS).

Let us now turn to the MSS. and learn what effect this Liquescence has on the form of neums.

The semivocal signs vary somewhat in form, as do the neums themselves, in each country, but in most cases the Liquescence is expressed by shortening the last stroke of a neum. In England, however, and in France, a contrary system prevails, and groups affected by Liquescence generally *lengthen* their last stroke.

Coming then to examine the semivocal Neums of the first class, we find that they are derived from the neum-accents by a simple modification of the last stroke of the sign. [1] (All neums may become semi-vocal, the *last* note being always the one affected.)

Neums ending in an acute accent are thus modified ;

ORDINARY NEUM.			LIQUESCENT NEUM.	
J	▌	becomes	◡	▌
N	◪	»	N	◪
/	◢	»	◡	◢
/./	▐◦▐	»	/◡	▐◦◢

Liquescent neums ending in a grave accent take the following form :

[1] See Plate 1.

e

ORDINARY NEUM.			LIQUESCENT NEUM.	
∧	⌐•	becomes	⁄	⌐
⋀	⊸•	ʺ	⌐	⊿
⌐⁄·	⌐••	ʺ	⌐	⌐ ⌐••
⌐·	⌐••	ʺ	⌐	⌐••

With regard to the Climacus, we must remember that the original
form of the neum was ⌐, and that ⁄· is a derived figure, though
very ancient. The Liquescent takes its shape from the original, uniting
in a curve the last two notes, both of which are semivocal ⌐. The
group thus changed is called *Climacus Sinuosus,* or Ancus, (ἀγκὼν =
curve). The Podatus when affected by Liquescence is called *Epiphonus,*
a corruption of Emiphonus, (ἡμίφωνος = semivocal), and the Clivis becomes Cephalicus, the shortening of the second stroke of the neum
making a kind of little head (κεφαλή). The other groups retain their ordinary name and are called, for instance, semivocal Torculus, Porrectus, etc.

II

We have already remarked that Liquescence is produced at times
by the *addition* of a note to the ordinary neum. In this case the semivocal note does not belong to the original melody, and it might be,
and indeed very often is, retrenched, without injuring the phrase. Neums
ending in an acute accent are more frequently affected by this kind of
Liquescence than those ending in a grave.

NOTATION OF LIQUESCENTS. (2ND. CLASS).

ORDINARY NEUM.				LIQUESCENT NEUM.		
Virga	/	¶	becomes	*Cephalicus*	↑	▮
Podatus	J	▮	»	*Liq. Torculus*	♪	▰
Scandicus	⸍	◢	»		⸍	◢
Porrectus	N	◣	»		N	◣
Torculus	⋀	⋔	»	*Pes sinuosus*	⌒	▮••
Climacus	/·.	¶••	»		/·.	◤
Pes subpunctis	J·.	▮••	»		J·.	◢◢

These additional notes, which are produced under the influence of the text, give a curious insight into Gregorian rhythm, showing both the freedom of its movements and its close union with the words. In fact the rules of this rhythm are strikingly portrayed in neumatic notation, and the liquescent neums furnish fresh proofs of the fact, and show that this notation is really a phonographic representation of the smallest details of Latin pronunciation. When taste had become depraved and execution heavy, these delicate shades were neglected and liquescent notes became a fruitful source of mistakes, and of serious alterations in the melody. The added liquescent note was sometimes taken for an essential note of the phrase, and itself received a liquescent addition. But in the best days of Gregorian Chant liquescent additions were made with exquisite taste and care, and served to embellish both rhythm and melody.

CHAPTER VI.

ROMANIAN SIGNS AND LETTERS.

The 4th. Vol. of the " Paléographie musicale " reproduces in facsimile a precious MS. belonging to the great Abbey of Einsiedeln (No. 121). It is a Gradual, noted throughout in neum-accents, and written at the end of the 10th. or the beginning of the 11th. century. The tradition of the Monastery, supported by a German inscription prefixed to the volume in 1599, assures us that it belonged to the Blessed Abbot Gregory. [1] (A. D. 945.)

The peculiar interest of this document lies in the Romanian Signs and Letters, which are added to the ordinary neumatic notation. In this particular, the MS. is the richest of its kind.

But what are these Romanian Signs and Letters? They have a history of their own which takes us back to the days of Charlemagne, and may here be told in a few words. The great King being at Rome for the Easter of 787, was called on to decide a dispute which had arisen between the royal and the papal singers. The King's cantors

[1] Mentioned in " Menology of England and Wales, " Nov. 13th. He is said to have been son of Edward the Elder, but however this may be, he was at least of the Royal family of England. Having left his country, he became a Monk in St. Gregory's Monastery in Rome, whence he passed to Einsiedeln, where he eventually became Abbot.

declared their preference for their own chants, while the Romans rested their claims to superiority on the authority of St. Gregory, whose teaching had been carefully preserved at Rome. The debate becoming animated, both parties referred the matter to the King. Having heard the arguments on each side, Charlemagne asked his followers : " Tell me, where is the stream the purest, at its source or in its channel ? " " In its source, " was the unanimous reply. " Then ", rejoined the King, " do you return to the source, for by your own argument you are proved to be in the wrong. " The practical result of the dispute was, that Charlemagne resolved to reform the Church Music in his dominions, and for this end obtained from Pope Adrian two cantors of the Gregorian School, each of them provided with an authentic copy of the Antiphonary. The cantors chosen for this mission were Peter and Romanus, who seem to have set out for Germany about the year 789. They travelled together as far as the great Monastery of St. Gall, where Romanus falling sick, Peter was obliged to continue his journey alone. He settled at Metz and founded there a school of sacred chant which flourished for many centuries.

On Romanus' recovery, the Monks, appreciating the treasure which Providence had entrusted to them, begged Charlemagne to leave the great cantor among them. The King consented, and Romanus spent the remainder of his life at St. Gall, forming a Gregorian Schola, and at his death he bequeathed his priceless Antiphonary to the Abbey. His experience as a teacher has happily left its mark. He must have had his full share of the difficulties inseparable from the training of a choir, and no doubt he found Northern voices more rebellious than the refined organs of his native land. In order to remedy the insufficiency of Neumatic Notation, as well as to mark various shades of expression, he added to the neums certain Signs and Letters, called after him " Romanian ".

There can be no doubt that Romanus himself was the originator of the system; we have the word of Ekkhard the Younger, Chronicler of the Abbey (1036) : " Primus ille (Romanus) in ipso Antiphonario litteras alphabeti significativas notulis, quibus visum est aut sursum, aut iusum, aut ante, aut retro, assignari excogitavit, quas postea cuidam amico quærenti Notker Balbulus dilucidavit ".

This letter of Notker's has happily been preserved, and has been published several times of late years, though so incorrectly as to be unintelligible in some parts. Fortunately there is an abridged form of the letter extant in a MS. of the 13th. century (St. Thomas', Leipzig.), which clears up the obscurities of the original. Notker's authority as interpreter of the Romanian Letters is unimpeachable, since the poet-monk was *almost* a cotemporary of the Roman master, if he had not actually found his way to St. Gall's in Romanus' lifetime. If he was not so fortunate as to hear the great cantor's lessons, he was at least instructed by his immediate disciples. As to its form, B⁴ Notker's letter does him no credit, being written in the worst style of that time. Instead of giving in simple terms the meaning of each letter, he goes out of his way and aims at beginning each word of his explanation with the letter under consideration. He succeeds in a few instances; but where he fails, he insists on getting at least the *last* word into his plan. This contrivance seriously endangers the clearness of his explanations, [1] but by the help of the Leipzig MS. the meaning of the most important letters has been ascertained.

---

[1] The following may give some idea of the perplexing effect of Notker's alliteration :

   g — Ut in *g*utture *g*radatim *g*arruletur *g*enuine *g*ratulatur.
   m — *M*ediocriter *m*elodiam *m*oderari *m*endicando *m*emorat.
   n — *N*otare, hoc est *n*oscitare *n*otificat.
   s — *S*usum, vel *s*ursum *s*candere *s*ibilat.

ROMANIAN LETTERS.

In order to appreciate the usefulness of these Letters we must remember that the Chironomic Notation to which they were applied was an imperfect system and had two serious deficiencies : it did not fix the intervals of the sounds, and it gave only scant indications as to rhythm and expression. Hence we find two principal classes of Letters, 1st. those relating to *intonation ;* 2nd. those relating to *rhythm*.

1st. CLASS.

LETTERS RELATING TO INTONATION. (7 LETTERS).

Of these, *four* indicate an *elevation* of voice, viz : —

      a — Ut *altius* elevetur admonet.

      l — Levare.

      ꜱ — Sursum.

      g — Gradatim.

Two denote a *lowering* of pitch, viz : —

      d — Deprimatur.

      i — Iusum or inferius.

One marks *unison,* viz : —

      e — equaliter.

2nd. CLASS.

LETTERS RELATING TO RHYTHM. (7 LETTERS).

One marks accelerando, viz : —

      c — celeriter or cito.

Three express ritardando, viz : —

      t — trahere or tenere.

      x — exspectare.

      m — mediocriter.

Three denote force or intensity, viz : —

> **p** — pressionem significat.
> **f** — cum fragore.
> **k** — clange or *Klenke*.

But Romanus' ingenuity goes still further, and we have another class of letters.

3RD. CLASS.

LETTERS MODIFYING THE PRECEDING. (3 LETTERS).

> **b** — bene.
> **v** — valde.
> **m** — mediocriter.

b and **v** are very frequently used to modify **t, i,** and other letters. **m** is found by itself, as in the 2nd. class, or with another letter, as **tm** — teneatur mediocriter.

Of all the letters **c** and **t** are the most frequently used, being found at almost every word in the MSS.

The remaining seven Letters are seldom or never used, though Notker takes the trouble to explain each of them.

As a rule the Romanian Letters, when added to a neumatic group, affect only *one* note ; for instance, in the following clivis 𝄇 the first note is long, while in this podatus 𝄈 it is the second. When a letter is to be applied to more than one note, it is drawn out over the group or groups, thus 𝄞𝄇. [1]

ROMANIAN SIGNS.

There are two classes of these Signs :

The first is formed by various changes in the form of the neum-

[1] For both Signs and Letters, see Plate 1.

accents, the lines being made longer or thicker, or being turned in different directions.

The *Punctum* (.) becomes . _

The first stroke of the *Podatus* (♩) is lengthened and makes ✓ or √

The *Torculus* (Λ) becomes .Λ or ∫

The *Porrectus* (N) becomes ∿

The *Climacus* (/·) changes its points into strokes and becomes /·. /·-. /·-. according to the number of notes affected.

The mark of the second class of Romanian Signs is the addition of a little stroke to the ordinary neum, or even to groups already changed as in the first class. Since this stroke may occupy various places in the groups, it is often obliged to change its form, so that we find it sometimes horizontal, sometimes curved, sometimes vertical; but, whatever its shape, it has always the same signification and denotes a lengthening of the note to which it is added. Unlike the signs of the first class, which mark the whole group as *ritardando*, this little stroke affects only one note, being repeated if applied to more than one.

The Romanian Sign is found in the following forms :

	ORDINARY NEUM.	NEUM WITH ROMANIAN SIGN.
Virga	/	⸍
Podatus	♩	♩
Clivis	Λ	Λ Ἃ
Torculus	⸍Λ	⸍Λ
Porrectus	N	N
Climacus	/·.	/·.
Scandicus	⸴/	⸴/

f

The importance of Romanian Signs and Letters can scarcely be exaggerated. Their authority is of the highest, since they are derived directly from Rome, through one of the most proficient Gregorian cantors of the 8th. century. They throw much light too on the practical execution of the chant, showing the manner of phrasing passages, marking *ritardando, accelerando, crescendo,* &c., with an attention to detail scarcely surpassed by our modern expression-marks.

We may remark in conclusion that these Romanian Signs and Letters, though originating at St. Gall's, are not confined to the MSS. of that house. They appear in the choir-books not only of the neighbouring Monasteries, but of distant places, and are found even in England.

———————

Having now some idea of the notation of the Gregorian melodies, we are prepared for the study of those melodies themselves. In seeking for the principle on which they are constructed, we must take the chants, not as they are in many modern editions, but as they appear in the most authentic MSS. ; just as the student of an ancient language turns to its most reliable monuments and reads its purest writers.

Our enquiry will therefore be concerned with the chants of the liturgical books in their ancient form, — (the Liber Antiphonarius, Liber Gradualis and Liber Responsorialis.)

The pieces contained in these books may be roughly classified as follows : 1st. *Antiphons* with psalm verses; i. e. Antiphons of the Office (Vespers, &c.), and of the Mass (Introit, Offertory, Communion.) — 2nd. *Responsories* of the Office (Matins), and of the Mass (Gradual), also followed by verses. (The Alleluia-verse belongs to this class.) — 3rd. *Tracts,* i. e. *verses* without Antiphons or Responsories.

There are then two distinct parts in liturgical pieces : (1) *Antiphons* and *Responsories* which open and close the chant of Psalms, — and (2) *Verses.*

Leaving aside Antiphons and Responsories, let us look at the melody of *Verses,* i. e. Psalms of the Office, and Verses of the Gradual of the Mass, and of the Responsories of Matins.

The first thing to strike us in psalm-tones is their simplicity. All Psalmody may be described as consisting of three parts. (1) *An intonation* ; — (2) *a reciting-note* (dominant) ; — (3) *cadences,* either medial or final. These forms serve to punctuate the phrase.

Di-xit Dó- mi-nus Dómi-no me- o : Se-de a   dextris me- is

The melody is more developed in the Psalms of the Introit, in the Psalm " Venite exsultemus, " and in the Verses of the Matins' Responsories ; yet we find the same component parts, — intonation, dominant and final. This we may call *ornate* psalmody. (e. g. Ps. I. M.)

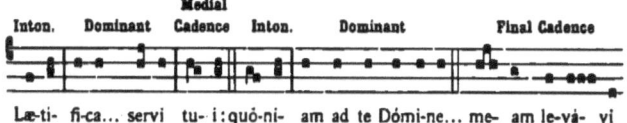

Læ-ti- fi-ca... servi tu- i : quó-ni- am ad te Dómi-ne... me- am le-vá- vi

Analysing *Tracts* and *Verses of Graduals* we find the same structure, though hidden under a greater number of notes and neums. This third style we may call *neumatic* psalmody. [1]

_____

[1] See Table at the end of this volume.

Tract.
VIII. Mode

Adjú-tor... faĉtus est mi-hi in sa- lú- tem

Psalmodic struĉture has, therefore, three parts, and each part, according as it is more or less developed, may belong to simple, ornate, or neumatic style. As far as construĉtion goes, a verse of a Traĉt, Gradual, or Alleluia may conceal under its florid neums a struĉture identical with that of a simple psalm-tone.

We may now enquire what is the *origin* of this Psalmody. — It is scarcely satisfaĉtory to be told that Psalmody comes from the Greeks, the Jews, or the Syrians. What we want to know is the *first,* the natural source of this musical declamation which we call Psalmody. This origin is not far to seek.

A little observation will discover that in the most natural and common form of speech a sentence begins on the lower notes of the voice, rises by degrees to a recitative, which varies according to the speaker's sentiments, and falls at the close, by well-prepared and pleasant cadences, to a final low note. These infleĉtions may be inverted under the influence of passion or great emotion, or for effeĉt, but the faĉt remains that a spoken phrase, in its *normal* state, consists of an *intonation*, a *recitative* (more or less varied), and a *cadence,* — three parts which we have already distinguished in psalmodic struĉture. May it not be found that Psalmody owes its origin to speech, and is really the musical expression of that speech? — And, to carry out the principle to the full, if the general form of a psalmodic phrase is borrowed from speech, may not Psalmody have likewise taken from language, (i. e. from the text of the Liturgy) its strong and weak notes, its accents, its divisions, its pauses, — in a word, all the details of its rhythm?

But, having advanced this supposition, we must, before trying to make it good, examine the charaĉteristics of Gregorian rhythm.

CHAPTER VII.

RHYTHM.

Rhythm (ῥέω, ῥυθμός), i. e. the flow of sound or language, " consists in the recurrence of accent or stress of voice[1] at regulated intervals. " " This regularity is made appreciable by a more or less symme-
trical division, into certain small portions, of the time occupied by a
musical or poetical work of art. Hence the word rhythm is applied to
the proportion, balance and symmetry between the various portions of
the composition. The Romans also applied the word to rhetorical compositions, having regard to the balance and symmetry of the sentences
and periods ; and this is the sense in which we have to apply it to Gregorian music. "[2]

There are two kinds of proportion and consequently two kinds of
rhythm.

" First there is *striâ* rhythm, (poetry and modern music) in which
the proportion is based on fixed and unchangeable rules.

" Then there is *free* rhythm, (prose) in which the proportion is
regulated by the natural instinct of the ear. "[3]

[1] This stress of voice is called *arsis*. and the unaccented syllable *thesis*.
[2] *Elements of Plain-Song*, p. 31.
[3] *Mélodies Grégoriennes*, ch. xiii.

Of this free rhythm, the oratorical " *numerus,* " Cicero says :
" Esse ergo in oratione numerum quemdam non est difficile cognoscere ; judicat enim sensus. Quod qui non sentiunt, quas aures habeant,
vel quid in his hominibus simile sit nescio. " [1]

In free, therefore, as in strict rhythm, there is a certain proportion,
consisting in the " balance and symmetry between certain portions of
the composition. " Such is Gregorian rhythm, — *free,* taking its form
from the text of the Liturgy and founded on principles of balance and
proportion and on the use of the *cæsura.* [2] This balance, says Guy of
Arezzo, consists primarily in the number of sounds and in the proportion of the pauses.

It would be beyond our present purpose to enter into a detailed
examination of these proportions ; the reader is referred to Dom Joseph
Pothier's exhaustive treatment of the subject, [3] and to the " Elements
of Plain-Song " in which the same principles are presented in an English
form.

Since the words of the Liturgical text are the " prima materies "
of Gregorian rhythm, and since the life of a word is its accent, " accentus anima vocis, " we may say that the tonic or acute accent is
the chief factor in this rhythm.

The first thing to remark about the tonic accent is its essentially
musical character. The syllable of each word which it affects was marked, with the ancients, by an elevation of voice, while the other syllables were in a lower pitch. The accent is really a *melody,* the expression of all that is most musical in language.

It seems however that this musical character belonged more to the

[1] Or. lv.
[2] *Elemenis*, p. 30.
[3] *Mélodies Grégoriennes*, ch. xiii.

Greek accent. Quintilian tells us that the Latin accent, though musical, had a certain force unknown to the Greek. In the Augustan Age, despite the efforts of literary purists, the accent gained in intensity, and by the third century it had obtained pre-eminence over the other syllables. It is important to observe that the accent by becoming strong became an element of rhythm in a word or a phrase, since rhythm consists in the alternation of strong and of weak beats.

This is not the place to write the history of the accent, but we may note that on the formation of the Romance languages, it further became *long;* indeed this lengthening of the accented syllable was one of the chief causes of the transformation and decadence of Latin. As a matter of fact, the long accent is not Latin at all, but a Romance, a modern accent. However, at the time in which we are interested, i. e. in the 3rd. and 4th. centuries, the accent was still *musical* and *strong,* and had not yet become *long*.

The *position* of the accent in Latin words is well known ; suffice it here to say that : 1st. in dissyllables the *penultimate* is accented : " *mitis, fórtis;* " 2nd. that in words of more than two syllables the accent falls on the *penultimate* if prosodically *long,* and on the *antepenultimate* if the penultimate is short : " *Redémptor, Dóminus.* "

These rules for the position of the accent bring out two important facts regarding the *melody* and the *rhythm* of Latin words. With regard to the first we remark that the musical elevation of the tonic accent on the penultimate or antepenultimate, occasions a fall of pitch on the following syllable or syllables of the word, so that the effect might be represented thus

Red-émptor   Red-émptor   Dómi-nus

As to the second fact, that which refers to the *rhythm* of words, — the *force* of the tonic accent falling always on the penultimate or antepenultimate, there is a consequent *weakening* of the subsequent syllable or syllables.

It follows from these indications that if, as we suppose, the tonic accent has had a real influence on the structure of Roman Psalmody, we should, as a general rule, find notes of higher pitch on the accented syllables and lower notes on the final syllables of words. Let us see whether the supposition is supported by the ancient MSS.

With a view to greater clearness, we purpose to confine ourselves to the *finals* of psalmodic phrases ; these cadences are, moreover, the most important parts of the phrase, — since it is at the end of a sentence or a period, whether musical or otherwise, that the rhythm is most strongly marked : " Cum aures extremum exspectent, in eoque acquiescant, id vacare numero non oportet. "[1]

But a word first on the *text* to which the melodies had to be fitted. The old Roman masters had no choice of words or phrases ; they had to take them as they found them in the prose-psalter, in which the cadences are very varied.

Let us see how the early composers set to work. Nothing could exceed the simplicity of their first expedient. This consisted in keeping to one reciting note until the last accent of the phrase inclusively, and then lowering the last syllable or syllables. This, the simplest inflection possible, occurs frequently in the Ambrosian Chant and occasionally in the Roman.[2]

---

[1] Cicero.
[2] See Table at end of this volume.

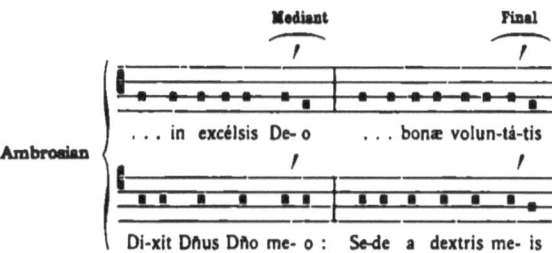

Or again, — and here the musical character of the accent is still further emphasized, — the melody rises on the acute syllable of the last word in a phrase, and falls again on the final syllable or syllables.

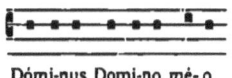

Dómi-nus Domi-no mé- o

The above examples are *cadences of one accent*. They give small enough scope to the music, and it is not surprising to find composers claiming more consideration for their art.

Acting always under the influence of the accent they begin their inflections on the last accent but one; examples may be found in the following final of 5th. mode, and in the mediant of the Introit psalms.

This is the cadence of *two accents*.

The melody still further asserts its rights in such pieces as the following which belongs to neumatic psalmody. The plain psalmodic construction is kept up until the last accent of the phrase, when the music, taking advantage of this accent, goes off into a long and joyous neum.

... ut palma flo-ré-   bit

These few examples, which might be multiplied *ad infinitum,* may suffice to show the influence of the tonic accent on the rhythm of psalmody.

So far we have traced that influence only in cadences of two or three notes. These forms are the most natural, the most akin to ordinary speech ; but our Gregorian composers did not overlook the *Cursus,* i. e. more studied combinations of accents and syllables. We shall see the masters making use of these forms, and composing more perfect melodies for these more perfect syllabic types. We must therefore recal the rules of the *Cursus.*

CHAPTER VIII.

THE " CURSUS. "

A " *Cursus* " is a certain harmonious succession of words and syllables, much used by prose-writers both Greek and Latin, with a view to procuring measured and pleasant cadences. When this combination of syllables is based on *quantity,* the Cursus is *metrical;* when on the tonic accent and the *number* of syllables, the Cursus is *rhythmical* or *tonic.* [1] It is with the latter that we are here concerned, since the text of the Liturgy is prose, and its rhythm, as we have seen, founded on the tonic accent.

There are *four* forms of the Rhythmical Cursus or Cadence. The first three are found in the prayer of the Angelus, with which we are all familiar :

1. Gratiam tuam, quæsumus... *nostris infunde*   Cursus planus.

2. Ut qui Angelo .   . incarnati- *onem cognovimus* Cursus tardus.

3. per passionem   . *gloriam perducamur* Cursus velox.

The fourth is exemplified in the following :

4. Deus qui corda   .   . illustrati- *one docuisti* Trispondiac Cursus.

[1] It is only since the 12th. century that the word " Cursus " has been used in the sense here attached to it.

These first examples demonstrate the use of the four Cursus in the prayers of the Roman Liturgy. In fact, we may open the Breviary or Missal at hap-hazard, and we shall be sure to find Collects, Secrets, Postcommunions, Prefaces, etc., ending in one of the four forms.

It will not be out of place to sum up the characteristics of these Cursus.

1st. CURSUS PLANUS. It consists of *five* syllables so disposed — a paroxyton[1] of three syllables preceded by another paroxyton :

5 syllables.

(be-   *nígnus il- lústra*
                              type : 2 + 3
(cle-   *menter ex- au di*

(mere- *amur in cǽ- lis*
                              equivalent to type : 2 + 1 + 2
(mun-   *demur in men-te*

This Cursus is called *planus*, says M. Noël Valois, on account of the monotony caused by the sequence of two words accented on the penultimate.

2nd. CURSUS TARDUS. This cadence of *six* syllables ends in a pro-paroxyton[2] of four syllables, preceded by a paroxyton :

6 syllables.

(solemni- *tá- te la- tí- ficas*
            carnis appa-ru it
                                     type : 2 + 4
(impi-   *o-rum oc-cu- buit*
(ini-   *mi-cos di- li-gere*
                                     Equivalents
(*méntis et córpo-ris*   2 + 1 + 3
(instau-   *ra-re di gnatus es*   2 + 3 + 1

---

[1] Paroxyton = a word accented on the *penultimate*.

[2] Proparoxyton = a word accented on the *antepenultimate*.

This Cursus is in fact only a Cursus planus lengthened, *retarded* by one syllable; hence perhaps its name.

3rd. CURSUS VELOX. Seven syllables. It ends like the preceding in a word of four syllables, but the word in this case is a paroxyton and is preceded by a proparoxyton of three or more syllables. Of the three Cursus this is the most solemn; it owes its name perhaps to the fact that it has more weak than strong syllables :

7 syllables.

præ- mi-a præstitisti	
pe- lagi li-beravit	type : 3 + 4
sanguine de-dicasti	
	Equivalents
Uni- *ge-ni-ti* tu-i vi-as	3 + 2 + 2
cernitur et in terra	3 + 1 + 1 + 2
pro- *fi- ciant* et sa-lu-ti	3 + 1 + 3

4th. The fourth form of the Cursus remains to be noticed; it is made up of *six* syllables thus arranged : A paroxyton of four syllables preceded by another paroxyton. This is the *Trispondiac Cursus :*

6 syllables.

a- *more roboremur*	
ter- rena modera-ris	2 + 4
duce revela-sti	

All the above cadences, in spite of their variety, have certain features in common, as the following table will show.

	1st. part.	Cœsura.	2nd. part.	
Cursus planus	/ .		. / .	5 syllables
» tardus	/ .		. / . .	6 »
» trispondiac	/ .		. . / .	6 »
» velox	/ . .		. . / .	7 »

" Each of the four Cursus is founded on two principal accents, and is thus cut up into two unequal parts separated by a cœsura which is marked by the distinction of the words. The first half always begins with an arsis or acute accent, and falls at the end of the word, v. g.
/   .   / ..
" *nostris, præmia.* " — This is the place of the cœsura. In the second half the movement is taken up again and after one or two syllables reaches the second accent, falling again on the final or finals; v. g.
. / . .   / ..   . . / .
" illustra, apparuit, dedicasti. "[1]

Turning to our musical cadences of five notes to which the last chapter had brought us, let us enquire whether they owe anything to the *Cursus planus,* which consists, as we have just seen, of five syllables.

Not to be rash, we may put the case thus : Is it possible to fit a literary *Cursus planus* to the musical finals of which we are seeking the origin? Would the result be perfect harmony between text and melody? Yes, most certainly. Take the following examples from the Preface (ferial tone); no one can fail to remark the coincidence of the acute accents of the words with the elevation of pitch in the melody :

[1] *Paléographie Musicale.*

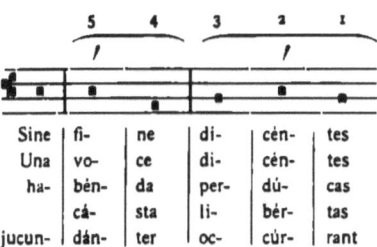

	5	4	3	2	1
Sine	fi-	ne	di-	cén-	tes
Una	vo-	ce	di-	cén-	tes
ha-	bén-	da	per-	dú-	cas
	cá-	sta	li-	bér-	tas
jucun-	dán-	ter	oc-	cúr-	rant

Is then the origin of these and similar musical phrases to be traced
to the Cursus planus? One is inclined to think so, from the relatively
large number of mediants and finals of five syllables to which the
Cursus planus lends itself so perfectly. These cadences occur at every
line in Sacramentaries, Graduals, and Responsorials, both Roman and
Ambrosian, and the pieces in which they are found belong to the three
classes of chant which we have already noticed (simple, ornate and
neumatic). The Pater, Preface, Exsultet, supply examples in *simple*
style, see the following :

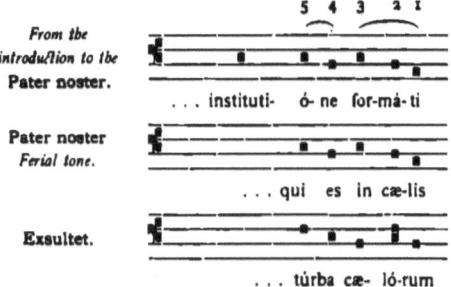

For pieces in *ornate* style we may refer to the *Introit* Ps. of all the
modes except the 5th., v. g. :

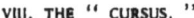
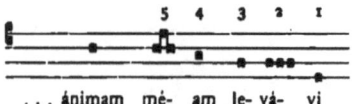

... ánimam mé- am le- vá- vi

For *neumatic* chants founded on the Cursus planus we may take
the Verses of the Matins' Responsories, in all the eight modes. [1]

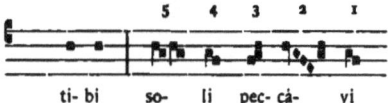

ti- bi   so-   li   pec- cá-   vi

    The structure is the same throughout. Adapt a Cursus planus to
any of the above cited cadences, and it will be seen that the melody
always rises to a higher note on the tonic accent and falls again on
weak syllables. Can this be accidental? It would indeed be strange,
were it so. A more reasonable conclusion is, that these innumerable
musical cadences were modelled by ancient composers on the literary
Cursus planus, just as the cadences of one or two accents, which we
have already studied, were formed on simpler types of speech. The
influence of the tonic accent on the structure of the Church's chant,
both in its melody and in its rhythm, is therefore evident.

    Yet, when all this has been said and insisted upon, and we turn
to the MSS. for justification of our theory, we find that the musical
cadences of five notes, which we have just been analysing, are not invariably so happy as to be fitted to the *Cursus planus.* We notice that
often enough, especially in florid cadences, the tonic accent of a word
is set to a lower note than are the unaccented syllables. Not only so,

                   [1] See Table at end.

but we find, *borribile dictu!* short, yes actually short penultimates en-
dowed with two, three, four, six or even more notes! What then is to
become of our fine theory?

Our authorities give several, and to our mind satisfactory, solu-
tions of this contradiction. We need not here dwell on the power of
the phrasing or logical accent; this accent is freer than the tonic accent,
which indeed it often overrules. Even in ordinary speech a word may
lose its usual accentuation under the influence of the logical or of the
pathetic accent. It is not surprising therefore that in Music, under the
same pressure, the tonic should lose its relatively higher pitch, or its
force, or even both.

A further explanation of our present difficulty may be found in the
consideration that a perfect agreement between text and melody, desirable as it is, admits of lawful exceptions, *whenever* the melody's form
or rhythm is so fixed as to give it a right to overrule the text. But of
this more presently.

These reasons might suffice, but there is another consideration
which is still more important and which goes to the root of the question. In studying our Gregorian melodies, we must be careful to dis-
criminate between the *original structure* of any given melody and the
adaptation of various texts to that same melody. The two questions
are quite distinct, and, in a certain sense, independent of each other. We
have already spoken of the *Origin* of a melodic structure, and may turn
in the next chapter to the question of adaptation.

But, before leaving the Cursus, we must say a word on its importance as a guide to fixing the *date* of our melodies. We are accustomed to hear that the restoration of St. Gregory's chant is impossible,
since we have no noted MSS. earlier than the 9th. century. True; but
is it fair to conclude that therefore the Chant itself cannot boast of any

h

greater antiquity? Is the time at which a MS. is written sufficient to fix the date of the composition of its contents? The logical conclusion of such reasoning would be that we must reject as spurious some of the greatest of St. Gregory's literary works, which come to us from the same century that gives us his chants. The famous " *Peregrinatio Sylviæ* " which is now interesting liturgical students, and which belongs to the 4th. century, has been recovered from an 11th. century MS. — This seems to show that there is some possibility of proving our chants to be authentic Gregorian ; but happily we have stronger arguments, furnished in part by the history of the Cursus.

The study of this literary formula has led to the conclusion that the *Cursus* was in use chiefly from the end of the 4th. to the middle of the 7th. century, from which time " rhythm seemed banished from prose for four centuries, " being restored only under B. Urban II (1088-99). This Pope's Chancellor, John Gaetani, was anxious 'o improve the style of the Roman Chancery and his efforts were not without success. The 12th. century welcomed several treatises, laying down the rules for this literary renaissance. Albert of Morra, who became Pope under the name Gregory VIII, (✠ 1187) wrote the " *Forma dictandi,* " a work which had so wide an influence that rhythmical prose began to be called " *stylus gregorianus* ". It was at this time that the terms " *Cursus velox, tardus,* and *planus* " came into use.[1] (The trispondaic Cursus was not then acknowledged). We will leave a learned writer in the " Correspondant "[2] to bring out the significance of these facts in their bearing on the Liturgical Chant. He remarks first — that a knowledge of the laws of the *Cursus* and of the date at which it

---

[1] See *Paléographie Mus.*, t. iv, p. 34.

[2] Décembre 1894. " Le Plain-Chant & le Pape S. Grégoire le Grand, " par M. Jules Combarieu.

fell into disuse makes this form a *precious criterion* for correcting a doubtful reading of a MS., and for proving the date or authenticity of certain charts ; just as a detail of dress, etc., may determine the period to which a statue belongs, or as the use of obsolete words may fix, at least approximately, the date of a literary work.

He then points out that the careful study of the *Cursus* has rendered an analogous service to Gregorian Chant, by throwing light on the vexed question of its authenticity. He says :

" There is a *musical* Cursus ; that is to say — there are in phrases certain cadences, in which the accented syllables are represented by higher notes, the unaccented syllables by lower notes. " He then sums up the reasoning of the " Paléographie Musicale, " as follows :

" In the Liturgical books of the three chief dialects of Plain-Chant (Ambrosian, Gregorian, and Mozarabic), we find more than a hundred cadences (repeated thousands of times) which follow the rhythmical rise and fall of the literary *Cursus planus* on which they have evidently been framed.

" Now we know that from the 8th. to the 12th. century there was a general disregard of the Cursus. This is the conclusion arrived at by M. W. Meyer, after studying numerous authors of all countries. M. Noël Valois, in his " Étude sur le rhythme des bulles pontificales, " shows that from the middle of the 7th. century the Cursus was scarcely observed, and often completely misunderstood.

" The Abbé L. Couture, on his side, bears witness that " from the time of St. Gregory the Great rhythm seems to have been banished for four centuries from literary prose. "

" The Gregorian Melodies may therefore be considered as contemporaneous with the literary formula on which they are built ; that is to say — their composition dates from before the middle of the 7th. cen-

tury. Now, St. Gregory's reign reaches just to the beginning of that
century, and therefore the Church is confirmed, by new titles, in her
traditional belief, " — the belief that her Chants are really the songs of
the early Church, gathered together, regulated, and enriched by Pope
Saint Gregory the Great.

CHAPTER IX.

ADAPTATION OF TEXTS.

We have already hinted at the difficulties in the task of organising Liturgical psalmody. Perhaps the most embarrassing question was how to secure perfect harmony between the text and the melody, and how to fit the various prose cadences of the Psalter to musical mediants and finals. There were only two ways out of the difficulty : one was to compose in each mode as many " motifs " or airs as there were syllabic combinations ; one, for example, for *Deus,* one for *Dominus,* one for *genui te,* etc., etc. This plan however entailed endless inconveniences ; if it would have procured perfect agreement between the words and the music, it would at the same time have destroyed the very character of psalmody, which ought to be, above all things, simple and popular. For we should have had a new musical formula, a new tune, or at least a change in the model-tune, at every verse of the Psalm. This was obviously impracticable.

The alternative which suggested itself and which was adopted, was — to choose among the endings of verses some simple and familiar types which might serve as models for all the cadence-melodies of the Psalter. All the syllabic endings, even when their accents did not agree with the type, would have to be adapted to the form chosen, on condition, however, of having the essential laws of their rhythm respected. This was the wiser and more practical plan.

The first syllabic types selected were naturally the simplest, as we have seen elsewhere : words of two syllables : *Déus,* — or of four : *Déus méus,* — and after these the *Cursus planus* : *méam levávi.*

It will be remarked that these three forms all end in a paroxyton. What then was to be done with a verse ending in a proparoxyton, e. g. *Dominus ?* What was to become of the additional short syllable which had to be fitted to the musical cadence, without altering its rhythm ?

In the case of simple cadences of one or of two accents (see p. 49) a solution was soon found by introducing an additional note for this short penultimate. The melody in these cadences is very light, we might say *elastic,* easily yields to the text, and can even receive additional notes without prejudice to its structure. [1]

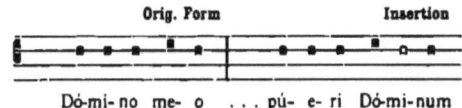

Orig. Form   Insertion

Dó-mi- no me- o   . . . pú- e- ri Dó-mi-num

With regard to cadences in *ornate* and *neumatic* style, the problem was more complicated. True, even in these the music is modelled on the accents of the text, and faithfully reflects the natural undulations of the voice ; but at the same time the melody is more developed, more impatient of the influence of the text ; it tends to fall back on its own great and varied resources, and to assert its inherent power. It is well to remember, in this connection, that the rhythm of a melody depends

[1] See Table at end.

not only on the words to which it is set, but also on the number of
notes, on their varied arrangement, on a proportion between the groups
of sounds. When therefore the music finds itself so hampered by the
text that it cannot freely express itself, it has no hesitation in asserting
its claims ; yet, even when it seems most independent, it has a thousand little ways of softening its demands, so as to leave as much influence as possible to the text and to preserve the unity of the words.

Let us look at one of the ingenious devices by which the melody
strives to keep on good terms with its neighbour, the text ; the first
example is from an Introit Psalm, *ornate* style.

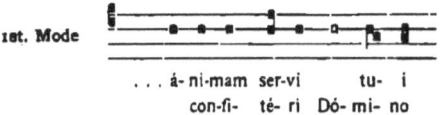

Here both tonic accent and musical rhythm are secured. The melody
insists on preserving the rhythm of this medial cadence and refuses to
insert a note for the penultimate between the last two groups, for such
an insertion would destroy the symmetry of the phrase. Cf. with above :

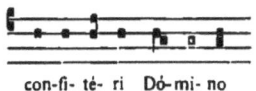

On the other hand, wishing to show some deference to the accent,
the melody doubles the first note of the clivis and draws the energy
of the accent on to that new note, which, by the force of its attack,
throws the following group on the short penultimate into the shade,
and causes it to be sung lightly and quickly. This is no arbitrary explanation, for the effect just described is marked in the Romanian MSS.

by the letter *c* (celeriter), placed over the clivis. — More could not be
done to ensure the predominance of the accent ; and as a matter of
fact, the pre-eminence of the melody in the above and similar examples is merely material and by a good execution would be rendered
unobservable. In spite of the *two* notes on the short penultimate the
whole form and rhythm of the melody come from the accent of the text.

Here is a second example of the same process, belonging also to
ornate psalmody, the verse of a Matins' Responsory.

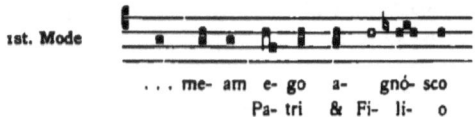

1st. Mode

. . . me- am e- go   a-   gnó- sco
           Pa- tri   & Fi- li-   o

This cadence brings before us a curious point in Gregorian rhythm,
and one which is closely connected with the question of short penultimates, — we mean *musical rhymes*. In the Gregorian and Ambrosian
chants there are real *musical rhymes* recurring frequently at the end of
phrases. When once the ear has become familiar with these forms, it
demands them in all their fulness, just as it requires the recurrence of
a rhyme or of a certain " foot " in poetry, or of a " cursus " in rhythmical prose. A beat more or less wounds the ear by producing a change
or hitch in the final.

Composers of old recognised the importance of these rhymes and
carefully respected them, shielding them, when needful, from the text's
encroachments. The process most generally adopted was the addition
of a note for the accented syllable, as we have seen in the two preceding examples.

We may examine another instance. Take the Introit : " *Populus
Sion* " for 2nd. Sunday in Advent, and that of the Octave-Day of
St. Laurence : " *Probasti me* ".

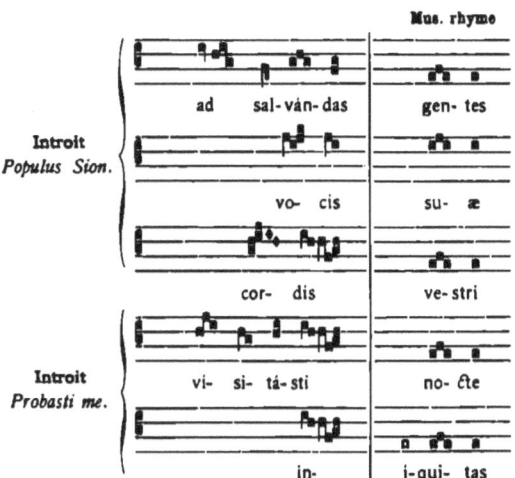

All the phrases of these two Introits end, in MSS., with the same musical rhyme on different degrees of the scale. With the words *gentes*, *suæ*, *vestri*, *noɛte*, there is no difficulty, the Torculus fitting in perfeɛt-ly with the accent. But lo! the last word in the last line is a propa-roxyton. Well, let it be; the Gregorian refuses to dislocate his *rhyme* and merely adds a note, *before* the Torculus, for the accented syllable. This form of cadence (♩♩ ♪) recurs at almost every line of chant and is a real rhyme. No ear, however slightly cultivated, or familiarised with the natural flow of this final, could bear the insertion of a note between the Torculus and the last note.

Faulty Cadence

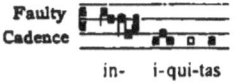

in-   i-qui-tas

To put it in a modern form, would not such an insertion be equivalent to a fourth quaver in a bar of $\frac{3}{8}$?

It is in order to avoid this unbearable dislocation, that composers employ the forms which we have noticed.

In the above cited examples we see the struggle between text and melody settled as it were by compromise, each yielding as much as possible to the other. But there are cases in which the music cannot but be inflexible and must overrule the words. This happens when a melody contains in itself all the formal elements of its own rhythm; or again, when it has taken its form so definitely from the original text for which it was made, that it can change neither the order nor the relative force of its notes and groups.

Take the following, from a Tract, 8th. Mode.

Tract.
VIII. Mode

. . . sa-   lû- tem
ju- di-   ci- um

This cadence has evidently been framed on " salutem, " or on a similar word; when a word ending in a dactyl presents itself at the cadence, it is fitted in just as it comes (see " *judicium* "), the *last three groups* to the *last three syllables,* whatever these may be.

Ornate cadences, formed on the *Cursus planus,* are treated in the same manner, the rule here being : *the last five groups* to the *last five syllables.*

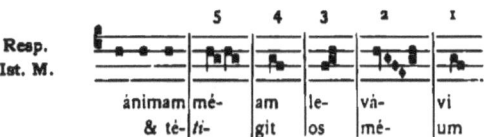

We are aware that these combinations are the horror of certain moderns, who do not hesitate to stigmatise our composers as ignorant barbarians. For our part, we agree with Dom Mocquereau in his reply to such objectors : " Without hesitation I take the side of these ' ignorant barbarians '; their names are St. Ambrose, St. Augustine, St. Leo, St. Gregory. I throw in my cause with the greatest literary men, rhetoricians, and grammarians of Greece and Rome, — with Dionysius of Halicarnassus, Longinus, Cicero, Varro, Quintilian, Marius Victorinus. Strange barbarians these men of talent, not to say genius ! Yes, they were keen connoisseurs in matters of style, of prose, and of poetry, but that did not prevent them from recognising in theory and in practice, that as often as a melody and its text are at variance, the music must take the precedence. ''

Their teaching on the subject is too clear to allow of misunderstanding. Let us take first a Greek, Dionysius of Halicarnassus. He says : " In music, whether vocal or instrumental, the words are subordinate to the chant and not the chant to the words. '' He gives as example a passage from a chorus in " Orestes, '' in which the music disregards the Greek accentuation.

Quintilian must speak for the Latins : " One is not allowed (in ordinary speech) to lengthen or to shorten words ; it is only Music that is thus free to make syllables either long or short at will. ''[1]

_____

[1] _Inst._, Or. ix, 4.

Turning to Mediæval theorists, we find the same principle insisted on. The author of the " *Instituta Patrum,* " after recommending attention to the proper pronunciation of words, adds this significant reserve : " as far as possible. "[1] The same writer says elsewhere that the fall of pitch in final cadences (when text and melody are at variance) is regulated not by the accent of the word but by the melody of the tone; and he adds, quoting Priscian : " Musica non subjacet regulis Donati, sicut nec divina Scriptura. "

Bernon of Reichnau is still more explicit and tells us that we are no more free to change a musical cadence fixed by tradition, than to accent the words " *docète et légite* " thus : *dócete et legíte* ; or to end an hexameter with a spondee and dactyl. He adds that if, for the sake of preserving the character of a melody, we change the usual value of a syllable, we must let grammarians grumble, and, with St. Augustine, follow the music which has a right to fix the rhythmical value of words.

There is then something to be said for the occasional pre-eminence of a melody over its text, for the use, v.g. of several notes on a short syllable. In fact, our composers, barbarians as they were ! showed much taste and esthetic sense in fully recognising not only the nature of musical rhythm, but also its demands, — its incontestable superiority, under certain circumstances, over the rhythm of language.

This need not surprise us. Music is employed for the sake of adding force to the words ; this implies that there is in it a power not to be found in mere speech. Why then should the text not yield occasionally to a melody from which it derives an increase of strength and beauty ?

---

[1] " In omni textu lectionis, psalmodiæ, vel cantus, accentus sive concentus verborum, *in quantum* suppetit facultas, non negligatur, quia exinde maxime redolet intellectus. " (Gerbert, *Scriptores*, t. i, p. 6-7.)

We willingly acknowledge that the perfection of the art is to secure absolute harmony between words and music. When, for example, a *Cursus planus* is fitted to a musical cadence formed on that syllabic type, nothing more perfect could be desired.

Yet, there are between text and melody relations which, though falling short of this desirable perfection, are full of charm. The musical cadences are so artistic in themselves, and appeal so strongly to the ear, that a change in any one of their parts would, in many cases, destroy the unity and beauty of the whole.

Generally, however, a melody is made to humour the varied texts to which it is fitted ; it is spread out, contracted or divided with wonderful facility, always with regard to the accent. The composers of these melodies considered *accentuation* the rule of rules. When therefore they seemed to disregard this rule, they acted thus not from ignorance or negligence, but from a true appreciation of their art and of its power. In fact, they resolved a question which is still a problem to musicians — the union of words and music.

CHAPTER X.

EXECUTION.

The reader who has followed this little work so far may be inclined to enquire : What is the practical outcome of such a study? What is its bearing on the execution of the chant? Has it anything to do with bettering the condition of our Plain-Chant choirs? Such questions are very natural, but to answer them fully would lead us far beyond the scope of the present work. We cannot, however, completely pass over this matter of execution, for it is all-important, and on it depends the reputation of the whole Gregorian system of song.

We give farther on the titles of a few practical works which every choir-master should study. Unfortunately there is little to be had in English, but we hope that this want may soon be supplied. For the present we shall confine ourselves to a rough sketch of the principles on which a Plain-Song choir should be trained.

What *kind* of execution is fitting for such melodies? Each style of music has its own style of execution and can have its full effect only when interpreted in that style. This is emphatically true with regard to Plain-Chant. We have tried to show that this venerable music is at once artistic and simple : artistic in its forms and principles, simple in the elements of which it is composed. Its execution must therefore be both simple and artistic; and the two qualities are not so difficult to reconcile as might at first appear.

By artistic we do not mean that all who attempt Plain-Chant must be *artistes*, nor do we say that a faultless voice is required; no, for experience proves that, with a moderate amount of training, very ordinary voices may attain to a most satisfactory rendering of Plain-Song. It must be owned that art of any kind has come to be an unknown quantity in most Gregorian services, and a more strange anomaly is scarcely to be found. There seems to be an idea not only that any kind of unprepared voice is good enough for Plain-Chant, but even that a cultivated singer should beware of " wasting his sweetness on such desert air. " There are people who will sing a song with careful attention to the rules of good taste, and who, on taking up a piece of Gregorian music, will perform it in the most unnatural manner, making it into a staccato exercise, or drawling out every note to an inordinate length, or again breaking up groups of notes in the most distressing manner. Surely a little art would be a boon here.

Firstly, the voice must be trained by exercises, in order to obtain both a sufficient volume of sound, and a true and precise " attack. " When this has been secured, the pupil should be practised in vocalise exercises, paying special attention to smoothness of execution and to purity of the vowel-sounds. (The vocalise should be sung to each vowel in turn). This attention to the mechanism of the voice is indispensable for acquiring a free and flowing movement in elaborate passages, as well as for accustoming the voice to the *legato* style, which is equally required in syllabic chant. Any approach to *staccato* must be carefully and constantly avoided, for nothing can be more painful than to hear the beautiful neums of a melody mercilessly jolted, with a new impulse of voice at each note.

These preliminaries may appear elaborate, and perhaps discouraging; but we repeat, they imply only a fair amount of training under an intelligent teacher, the *sine qua non* of advance in any art. Let the attempt but be made, and the result will surprise. It has been tried with complete success in not a few places, where simple choirs composed of men and of boys, trained generally by their Priest, succeed in rendering the Gregorian melodies in a satisfactory manner. What then might not be done with more artistic elements? It is not too much to ask for some cultivation of a voice which is to sing God's praise, for surely that, if anything, should be done to the best of one's power. The Holy Scripture praises David not merely for " *setting singers before the Altar,* " but for " *making sweet melody in their voices.* " The long, persevering practice of the world's singers may well shame us into doing the little that is needed to fit ourselves for so holy a work. Moreover, when once the chant with its rhythm has been fully grasped, a great amount of practice is unnecessary; the airs are very " catching, " and even children soon learn to sing them by heart.

As to the simplicity which we have said is the second characteristic of a good execution, it follows from the very nature of Plain-Song. This musical system owes its existence to the Liturgical text; " Its *rôle* is to unite itself with the words of the Church's prayer, so as to give them their full expression. " The words are the soul of this melodic body; they give it life. This is the chief axiom which we have tried to develop in the preceding pages.

Practically, the important point to remember is that in Plain-Chant *the notes have no value of their own,* but only *that of the syllables to which they are sung.* This is the fundamental rule : " *Cantabis syllabas sicut pronuntiaveris,* " that is to say : " Sing as you would speak. " This rule is easiest of application in syllabic pieces, in those, i.e. in which generally *one* note corresponds to each syllable. An excellent plan for teaching such pieces is to make the pupils read the text, taking care to give the proper accentuation, not only to each word, but to the piece as a whole ; the places of the pauses, whether longer or shorter, should also be pointed out. When the pupils have succeeded in reading the text satisfactorily, they should be made to *sing* it, keeping in singing exactly the same movement as in reading, for such portions of the chant are really gems of modulated reading.

The whole execution of syllabic chant may be summed up in two rules : 1st. Mark well the accents of words and phrases, and 2nd. Observe the various pauses according to the sense of the text. [1]

Elaborate, or what we call *neumatic* chants, are treated on the same principles as simpler melodies. Here again the greatest care must be taken to give the words their full force by bringing out the accented syllable. This is the less easy on account of there being on each syllable a number of notes, and a certain amount of skill is required for preserving the unity of the words.

When, as sometimes happens, an unaccented syllable bears a number of notes, and the tonic syllable only *one*, the full power of the accent must be given on that one note and the rest of the word sung lightly. It cannot be too strongly impressed on the reader that the force of accentuation depends not on the *number* of notes, nor on the *length* of a note, but on the *stress* laid on the syllable which is to be accented.

We saw in a previous chapter (Chap. iv, p. 24) how carefully the traditional manner of grouping the notes was preserved, even up to a late date. Attention to this *grouping* is essential for an intelligent rendering of Plain-Chant. The rhythm of a passage may be completely

---

[1] The Antiphons of the Office are in syllabic style, as is also the *Credo*, and sometimes the *Gloria in excelsis*.

disfigured by ignorance or carelessness in this matter ; if, for example, groups written apart be joined in singing, or *vice versa ;* or again, if an insignificant note be so sung as to make it important, or if an important note be put in the shade. Those who are unfortunately obliged to make use of choir-books in which the grouping of the sounds has been disregarded, cannot do better than compare their books with one printed in traditional notation, and follow as far as possible with their mutilated melodies the rhythmical indications there given. These details may appear to be mere minutiæ, but they are some of the little things on which perfection depends.

With regard to these groups, the chief rule to be observed is, that all notes *printed* closely together are to be united in *singing*. Each group is considered in some sort as one note, and must be sung with one impulse of voice. Again, the *first* note of each group should be accented (but not lengthened), and the other notes of the group should flow from this initial impulse. Tailed notes generally have an accent, not because they are tailed, but because their position usually requires that they should be well marked. On the other hand, diamonds are not to be hurried over, since they are equal in value to the tailed notes, but they should be sung lightly, and should be dependent on the accent given to the tailed note which precedes them.

The neums of the florid pieces of chant are extremely graceful and beautiful ; they require a light, easy, flexible execution, without which their grace and beauty are as though they were not. To do them justice it is important that the singer should know how to control his breath, and one aim of the preliminary exercises is to strengthen the lungs and to gain full command in this respect. The power of sustaining is a great advantage, but sometimes even the longest breath may require a new impulse in singing a word. When this occurs, strict attention must be paid to what a mediæval musician calls " *The Golden Rule,* " — an elementary and most natural rule, but one which is sadly neglected : breath must never be taken immediately *before* a new syllable *in* a word. " Non debet fieri pausa, quando debet exprimi *syllaba incboatæ* dictionis. " So that in a vocalise such as the following, one may take breath at 1 or 2 but on no account at 3.

As to the speed at which the chant should be sung, the extremes of drawling and of hurrying are to be avoided. Some authorities give 132 Metronome as a guide, but much depends on the spirit of the piece and on the size of the Church. — In the course of each piece good taste will suggest changes of speed. Every pause should be prepared by a *ritardando,* and this slackening of speed must be in proportion with the length of the pause which is to follow ; a short pause will require only the last of the preceding notes to be slightly prolonged, a medium pause will suggest a fuller preparation, while the final of a piece will demand a considerable *ritardando*. It is almost unnecessary to say that attention must be paid to shades of expression ; it is not human to sing a piece through at an uniform loudness. As a rule the accented syllables, in both neumatic and syllabic chant, should be louder than the other syllables of a word ; — all *final* phrases should be sung softly.

Attention to the above-cited rules will secure a proper *expression*. This expression, that it may be in keeping with the Gregorian style of music, must be simple and natural, without even a suspicion of affectation or self-seeking. Plain-Chant does not depend for its expression on far-fetched effects; the sacred text has within itself the elements of this expression. Above all there must be nothing suggestive of a theatrical manner of singing. The Fathers of the Church, and Saints, and Bishops, up to the present day, have been severe in banishing all such worldly reminiscences from the Sanctuary. In England, as early as the 8th. century, we have a Synod speaking strongly on abuses of this kind.[1]

Such exaggerations have however nothing to do with the cultivation of the voice which we have been advocating. Art is necessary here, " not to supply resources to artificial sentiment, but to prepare a docile instrument which will give facility of expression to real sentiment. "

To sum up, let us remember that, to secure a proper execution and expression, it is absolutely necessary (1) that the words of the text be correctly pronounced and grouped; (2) that the rhythm be regularly kept up; and, though last not least, that the singers fulfil their task with piety.

If, together with the preparation of which we have spoken, the singer's whole soul be thrown into the chant, then Plain-Song will infallibly have its full expression.

We may add that the accompanist is to a large extent responsible for the execution of Plain-Song, for although accompaniment is merely an accessory, it exercises considerable influence on the chant, for either better or worse.

A great deal has been said and written on the proper manner of accompanying Gregorian Chant, but much discussion may be dispensed

---

[1] " Ut presbyteri sæcularium poetarum more in ecclesia non garriant, ne tragico sono sacrorum verborum compositionem ac distinctionem corrumpant vel confundant, sed simplicem sanctamque melodiam secundum morem ecclesiæ sectentur. "

(Synod of Clovesho, A.D. 747. Canon xii.)

with, when once it is agreed, that the perfection of any accompaniment is, to be in strict agreement with the melody which it is to support. The best accompaniment, that which fully bears out its name, does not aim at leading the voices, in an obtrusive manner; still less at drowning them in its magnificence. It is content to give a sympathetic support to the singers, and to suggest more than it expresses.

It is generally agreed that in accompanying Plain-Song the harmonies should be founded on the Diatonic Scale. Chromatic progressions are absolutely foreign to the Gregorian melody, and rob it of many of its strongest and most beautiful effects. Strict attention should be paid to the modality of each piece. The accompaniment should moreover " be small in volume and very simple in texture, the parts moving as *little* as possible and as small intervals as may be; for every large interval (more especially in the bass) tends to make it *sound* heavy, and actually makes it difficult to avoid playing heavily, thereby hampering the freedom of the rhythm. " [1]

A *loud* accompaniment is to be strongly deprecated, as most prejudicial to a choir, since it obliges the singers to exert themselves, probably beyond the strength of their voices, and thus causes a strained effect which is both disagreeable to the audience and hurtful to the performers.

The *stillness* of the parts noted above should be observed in accompanying Psalmody as well as elaborate pieces. Some organists seem to look on the Psalms as a delightful opportunity of escaping from the exigencies of the choir, and of exhibiting their proficiency in scale-passages. Yet experience proves that a calm accompaniment, varied by a judicious change of chords, affords the most satisfactory setting for Psalm-tones.

[1] *Elements of Plain-Song.* p. 90.

The organist must be thoroughly conversant with the theory of the Chant which he is to accompany. If he be himself accustomed to *sing* it, so much the better, for he will then have regard to details which only practical experience can appreciate. He must, moreover, be careful to mark the rhythm of each piece, bringing out its accents, and passing lightly over unaccented notes and phrases.

But besides correctness of harmony and of execution there is in good accompaniment a something, difficult indeed to define, but easy to feel, the absence of which is often fatal to the performances of even the best-trained choirs : — this is that sympathy, without which accompaniment can be only a hindrance. The organist must be in touch with his choir; he must feel for its weaknesses and be ready to give support, he must know its strong points and give them scope, and he must be willing to restrain those gorgeous harmonies which too often seduce the accompanist of Plain-Song.

In conclusion, we venture to express a hope that these simple pages may induce some of our readers to apply seriously to the study of Gregorian Music, or may be of service to those whose duty and privilege it is to spend their life in choral praise. We should consider ourselves happy if we might contribute in any degree to furthering the intelligent celebration of the holy Liturgy, or to increasing an appreciation of the artistic and devotional merits of Plain-Song, so that our choirs might realise that word of the great Patriarch St. Benedict : " *Mens nostra concordet voci nostræ.* "

MUSICAL EXAMPLES.

Introit.

O S ju- sti me-di- tá- bi-tur sa-pi- én-ti- am, &

lingua e- jus loqué-tur ju-di- ci- um : lex De- i e- jus in

corde ipsi- us. *T. P.* Alle-lú- ia, al-le- lú- ia. *Ps.* No-li

æmu-lá-ri in ma-lignànti-bus : neque ze-lá-ve-ris fa-ci- éntes in-iqui-

tá-tem. Gló-ri- a Patri, & Fi-li- o, & Spi-ri-tu- i Sanĉto. Sic-ut

e- rat in princi-pi- o, & nunc, & semper, & in sæcu-la sæcu-ló- rum.

Amen.

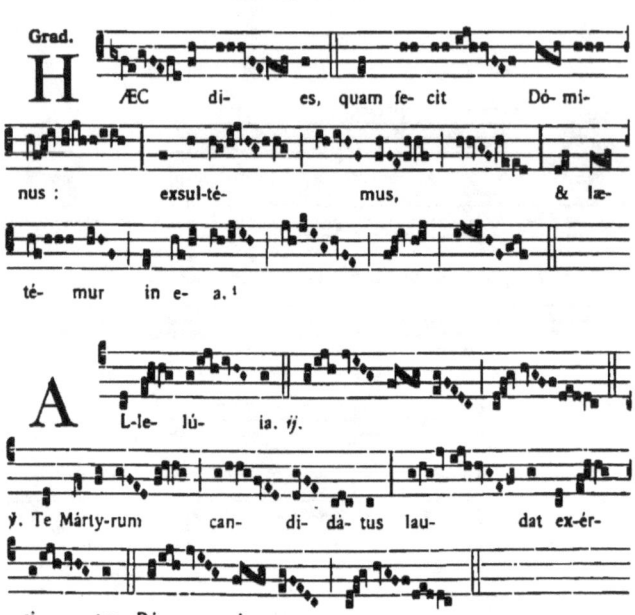

Grad.

HÆC di- es, quam fe- cit Dó- mi-

nus :   exsul-té-   mus,   & læ-

té- mur in e- a. [1]

ALle- lú- ia. *ij.*

℣. Te Márty-rum   can-   di- dà- tus lau-   dat ex-ér-

ci-   tus, Dó-   mi- ne.

[1] For the melody of this Gradual see Plate 5.

We give a list of works in which the statements of the preceding pages may be verified :

" PALÉOGRAPHIE MUSICALE. " Les principaux manuscrits de chant Grégorien, Ambrosien, Mozarabe et Gallican, publiés en fac-similés phototypiques par les RR. PP. Bénédictins de Solesmes. Recueil trimestriel, 25 fr. par an.

" GRADUALE SARISBURIENSE. " Fac-simile of a 13th. century Gradual, published by the " Plain-Song and Mediæval Music Society. " (B. Quaritch, London).

" LIBER GRADUALIS " juxta antiquorum codicum fidem restitutus. — Editio altera. (Solesmes, 1895.)

" LIBER USUALIS MISSÆ ET OFFICII CUM CANTU GREGORIANO. " (Solesmes, 1896). This is an invaluable little volume, serving the purpose of Missal, Gradual, and Vesperal. It contains, besides all the prayers and chants of the Ordinary of the Mass, the complete proper (Mass and Vespers) for all Sundays and Double feasts, the whole office of Christmas-Day and Holy Week, and the Office of the Dead. All this is comprised in a volume of convenient dimensions and of an equally convenient price.

1

For practical purposes, the following will be found useful.

" ELEMENTS OF PLAIN-SONG. " H. B. Briggs. (Quaritch, London. 1895.)

" MÉTHODE PRATIQUE DU CHANT GRÉGORIEN, " par Dom A. Schmitt. (Solesmes.)

" GRAMMAIRE ÉLÉMENTAIRE DE CHANT GRÉGORIEN, " par le Chan. Cartaud. 2nd. Edition. (Solesmes, 1896.)

" LE MÉCANISME VOCAL DANS LE CHANT GRÉGORIEN, " par A. Vigourel, Prêtre de S. Sulpice. o fr. 20.

APPENDIX.

I. THE MODES.

The question of gregorian modality being so important, some surprise may be felt at our having merely alluded to it. The omission is, however, voluntary, for the matter still awaits further study. As it is now engaging the attention of musical students, we trust that their labours may result in elucidating a subject as important as it is at present obscure. In the meantime, we give here, for the convenience of our readers, the current theory of gregorian modes, though it is doubtful whether the system will prove ultimately tenable.

———————

Eight modes are recognised in gregorian chant. These eight modes are comprised in four scales of an octave each, beginning respectively on the notes, *re, mi, fa, sol.*

It must be borne in mind that in Plain-Chant only the *diatonic* scale is admitted, hence the four scales of which we speak do not correspond to the modern scales of the same tonic. All the notes of our four scales are natural, and the distinguishing feature of each octave is the position occupied in it by the semitones.

Each scale consists of two tetrachords, thus arranged : [1]

1ST. TETRACHORD.	2ND. TETRACHORD.
re mi fa sol	la si ut re
mi fa sol la	si ut re mi
fa sol la si	ut re mi fa
sol la si ut	re mi fa sol

To each of these scales belong *two* modes which agree as to their *final*, but differ as to their *dominant*.[2] The first of each pair of modes is called *authentic* or *primitive*; the second, *plagal* or *derived*. In the plagal modes the order of the two tetrachords is reversed, so that the scales of those modes are sometimes said to be, *la, si, ut, re*.

TABLE OF MODES.

Nº	NAME	FINAL	DOMINANT	CHARACTER
I.	Authentic	re	la	Gravis
II.	Plagal	re	fa	Tristis
III.	Authentic	mi	ut	Mysticus
IV.	Plagal	mi	la	Harmonicus
V.	Authentic	fa	ut	Lætus
VI.	Plagal	fa	la	Devotus
VII.	Authentic	sol	re	Angelicus
VIII.	Plagal	sol	ut	Perfectus

[1] The place of the semitones is marked by a slur.
[2] Not to be confounded with the *dominant* of the modern scale. In Plain-Song the dominant is really the *predominant* note in each mode.

In the authentic modes the melody often embraces the higher notes of the scale, and hardly ever falls below the final. In the plagal modes, on the contrary, the melody seldom rises above the dominant, and a great part of it may be below the final.

These remarks cannot, however, be rigidly applied, for some pieces partake of two different modes, and these two modes need not be the relative authentic and plagal. The melody, again, often passes from one mode to another in a manner very much akin to modulation from key to key. [1]

[1] See " The Winchester Troper, '' edited by R. W. Howard Frere for the Henry Bradshaw Society. 1894. Introduction, p. xxxvii. — Plate 2 of our volume reproduces a page of this Troper.

II. PSALMODY.

Psalmody comprises the chant of the psalms and of the canticles of the Liturgy. [1]

Psalms are divided into verses, and each verse consists of two distinct parts marked in the liturgical books by an asterisk (*).

There are eight regular psalm-tones, one for each mode, and one irregular tone called *Tonus peregrinus*.

THE EIGHT PSALM-TONES.

First Tone.

[1] The following pages are taken from the " Petit Traité de Psalmodie " just completed by the Solesmes Fathers, and kindly put by them at our disposal. The treatise is a preface to the noted Psalter which is to appear shortly. In this work the purest traditions of psalmody have been restored, and several unwarranted exceptions, formerly in vogue, have been suppressed. We hope to translate the " Traité " in full, together with a Method of chant now in preparation.

Second Tone.

Third Tone.

Fourth Tone.

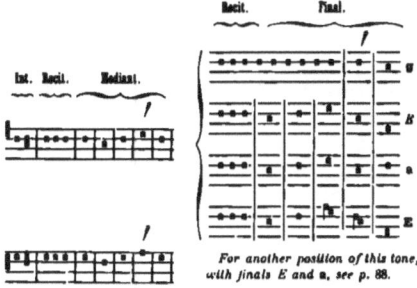

*For another position of this tone,
with finals E and a, see p. 88.*

Fifth Tone.

Sixth Tone.

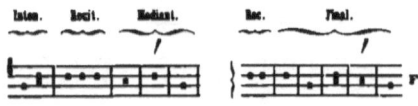

Seventh Tone.

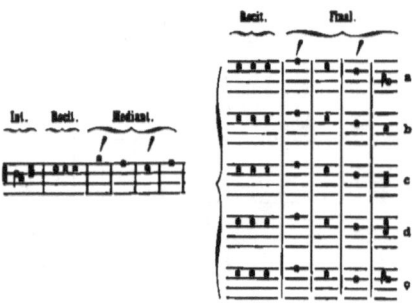

Eighth Tone.

Tonus *Peregrinus*.

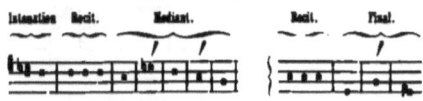

Fourth Tone transposed.

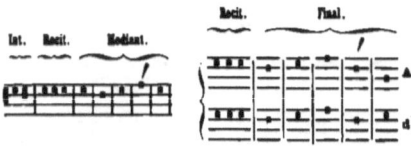

It will be seen from the above tables that every complete Psalm-tone consists of : (1) Intonation, (2) Recitative, (3) Cadences, either *medial* or *final*.

I. INTONATION.

The Intonation is a musical formula connecting the final phrase of an antiphon with the dominant of the psalm-tone which follows. It is used for only the first verse of every psalm, and for each verse of the Gospel-Canticles (*Magnificat, Benedictus,* and *Nunc dimittis*).

The *intonation* consists of two or three notes or groups, which are adapted to as many syllables. There is no exception to this rule. The syllables must be fitted in just as they come, and the groups of notes may not be disunited.

The intonation of the *Magnificat* follows the ordinary form in the 1st., 3rd., 4th., 5th. and 6th. modes; in the other modes it is as shown below.

m

In the 2nd. and 8th. modes, the usual form of intonation is used for all the verses except the first.

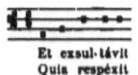

Et exsul·távit
Quia respéxit

II. RECITATIVE.

The recitative comprises all the notes in unison between the intonation and the mediant, and from the mediant to the final.

In the eight regular tones the recitative is always the dominant of the mode. The irregular tone (Tonus Peregrinus) has two recitatives; *la* for the first half of the verse, and *sol* for the second.

In the choir-books of the monastic rite, the recitative of verses of unusual length is broken by the *flex,* the sign of which is a cross (†). This flex is made by lowering the syllable or syllables following the last accent. In the 1st., 4th., 6th., 7th. and Peregrinus tones, the fall is of a major second; in the other tones, it is of a minor third.

III. CADENCES, (MEDIANTS AND FINALS).

NUMBER OF CADENCES.

Medial cadences end the first half of a verse. There is *one* such cadence for each mode. (See Table, p. 86). *Final cadences* end the second half of a verse; they are more numerous than medial cadences. The reason of this is to be found in the connection which exists between a psalm and its antiphon. The ending of the antiphon is connected, as we have seen, with the intonation of the psalm; in the same way, the ending of the psalm prepares for the repetition of the antiphon. As, however, there are various manners of beginning antiphons, the endings of the psalm-tones are modified to suit the different forms of intonation.

To mark which of the endings is to be used, letters are prefixed to the antiphon :

	la	si	ut	re	mi	fa	sol
Capitals	A	B	C	D	E	F	G
Small letters	a	b	c	d	e	f	g
Modified letters	à		ç		E		

A word on the signification of these letters. Capitals are used if the last note of the ending is also the final note of the mode. Small letters are employed when the psalm-tone ends on any note except the final of the mode. If, in any mode, two psalm-tones end on the same note, modified letters are used.

The melodies of the psalm-cadences being unchangeable, and, at the same time, having to be applied to the most various combinations of syllables, it might seem a thankless task to attempt any classification of these forms. But such is not the case. For practical purposes it is sufficient to follow the rules of Latin accentuation, modified occasionally by the rules of rhythmical poetry.

In Latin the accent falls, in dissyllables, on the first syllable, *fórtis*. In words of more than two syllables, the accent occurs on the penultimate if long, and on the antepenultimate if the penultimate is short : *manére, discípulus*.

The psalm-tones may be divided into two classes : those founded on *one* accent, *méo*, and those founded on *two* accents, *córde méo*. [1]

$$25 \text{ cadences of } one \text{ accent} \begin{cases} 5 \text{ mediants} \\ 20 \text{ finals} \end{cases}$$

$$10 \text{ cadences of } two \text{ accents} \begin{cases} 4 \text{ mediants} \\ 6 \text{ finals} \end{cases}$$

[1] See p. 49, and the Table at end.

m*

II. PSALMODY.

CADENCES OF ONE ACCENT.

ı. MEDIANTS (Fıvɛ).

Passing from recitative to accent

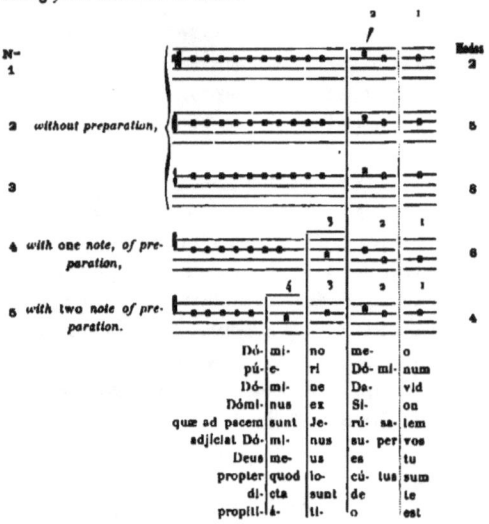

ii. FINALS (Twenty).

We give four of these finals adapted to verses of various lengths.

Passing from recitative to accent

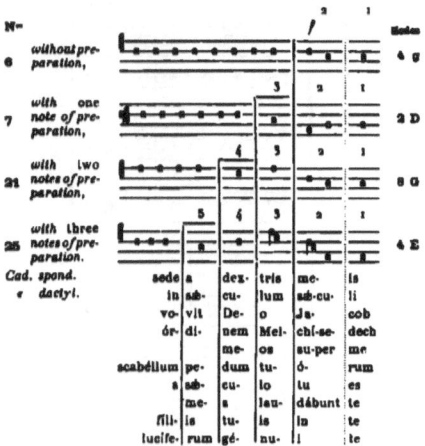

			sede	a	dex-	tris	me-	is
			in	sub-	cu-	lum	sub-cu-	li
			vo-	vit	De-	o	Ja-	cob
			ór-	di-	nem	Mel-	chí-se-	dech
					me-	os	su-per	me
	scabéllum		pe-	dum	tu-	ló-	rum
		s	sub-	cu-	lo	tu	es
			me-	s	lau-	dábunt	te
	fili-	is	tu-	is	in		te
	lucife-	rum	gé-	nu-	i		te

RULE. **A.** The penultimate or antepenultimate syllable of each verse or half-verse, must correspond with the accent of the melody. — **B.** The notes preceding the accent are set each to one syllable. In these cadences the rhythmical formula begins on the accent; the preceding notes are a graceful preparation leading to the accent, and therefore should not be overladen with syllables. (As some cadences of one accent pass directly from the recitative to the accent, there is no occasion in such cases for applying the second half of the preceding rule).

Cadences without preparation, Mediants of the 2nd., 5th. and 8th. modes, and final of the 4th. mode, (g).

Cadences with one note of preparation, Mediant of the 6th. mode, and finals of the 2nd. (D), 3rd. (c, à), and irregular modes.

Cadences with two notes of preparation, Mediant of the 4th. mode, and finals of the 1st. (f, g, a, à, D, J), 3rd. (a, g, E), 6th. (f), and 8th. (G, c) modes.

Cadences with three notes of preparation, Finals of the 4th. mode (*E*, a, E).

CADENCES OF TWO ACCENTS.

I. MEDIANTS (Four).

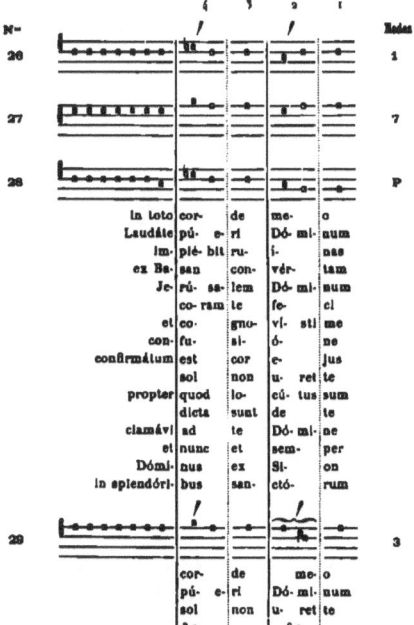

in toto	cor-	de	me-	o
Laudáte	pú- e- ri	Dó- mi- num
im-	plé- bit	ru-	i-	nas
ez Ba-	san	con-	vér-	tam
Je-	rú- sa- lem	Dó- mi- num
	co- ram	te	fe-	ci
et	co-	gno-	ví- sti	me
con-	fu-	si-	ó-	ne
confirmátum	est	cor	e-	jus
	sol	non	u- ret	te
propter	quod	lo-	cú- tus	sum
	dicta	sunt	de	te
clamávi	ad	te	Dó- mi- ne
et	nunc	et	sem-	per
Dómi-	nus	ex	Si-	on
in splendóri-	bus	san-	ctó-	rum

	cor-	de	me-	o
	pú- e- ri	Dó- mi- num
	sol	non	u- ret	te
	&c.		&c.	

II. FINALS (Six).

N°		4	3	2	1		Modes
30	*(musical staff)*						5 a
31	*(musical staff)*						7 a
32	*(musical staff)*						7 b
33	*(musical staff)*						7 c
34	*(musical staff)*						7 d
35	*(musical staff)*						7 ç

	4	3	2	1
sede a	dex-	tris	me-	is
in	seb-cu-	lum	seb-cu-	li
scabéllum	pe-dum	tu-	d-	rum
	O-	reb	et	Zeb
Ja-	cob	et	Jo-	seph
	l-	era-	el	est
Isra-	el	in	Dó-mi-	no
pax	su-	per	l-era-	el
	us-que	in	seb-cu-	lum
	ad-huc	sum	te-	cum
	e-	qui-	tá-	te
	com-	mo-	vé-bi-	tur
in-	i-	qui-	tá-	tem
justifi-	ca-	ti-	ó-ni-	bus
confirmátum	est	cor	e-	jus
	qui	cu-	stó-dit	te
	et	in	ter-	ra
órdi-	nem	Mel-	chi-se-	dech
sustinu-	l	te	Dó-mi-	ne
vólu-	cres	pen-	ná-	læ

RULE. The last two accented syllables of the verse or half-verse, must correspond with the two accents of the melody. It is not allowed, however, to seek the first of these two accented syllables beyond a certain limit; that is to say, one may not go back more than three syllables from the *last* accent of the verse.

SOLEMN TONE OF THE MAGNIFICAT.

(Ornate cadence of one accent.)

There is a more solemn chant for the Magnificat, in the 1st., 2nd. and 8th. modes. This is sung *ad libitum* on greater feasts.

RULE. The last accented syllable of the verse must be sung to the accent of the tone (col. 2.) The groups or notes of col' 3, 4, 5, must be fitted to the three syllables preceding the last accent.

1430. — Solesmes. Printed at St. Peter's Press. January 1897.

		Intonation	Dominant	Medial C
Simple Psalmody	Ambrosian	A		Glór-ri-a in excélsis	Dé- o
		B		Dixit Dóminus Dómino	mé- o
	Roman	C	Dixit Dó-	minus Dómino	mé- o
	Simple Preface	D	creatúra libe-	ra ab omni impugna-	tóris in- cúr- su
Ornate Psalmody	Psalms of the Introit	E	Læti- Bonum	fi-ca ánimam est confi-	sérvi té- ri tú- i Dómi-no
	Verses of the Responsories	F	Quóni- am	In-iqui- tá- tem mé- am ego a- Patri et	gnósco Fí- li- o
Neumatic Psalmody	R.-G. Justus	G	Ju-	stus ut palma flo-	ré- bit
		H	Si me- i	non fú- e-rint do- mi-	ná-
	Tract	I	Adjú-tor	et pro- té-ctor fá-ctus est mi- hi in sa- ju- dí-	lú- tem ci- um
	Alleluia	J	Di- es	sancti- fi- cá- tus il- lú- xit	nó-
	Tract	K			

Cadence	Intonation	Dominant	Final Cadence		

Et in ter- ra pax ho-mí- nibus bonæ vo-lun- tá- tis **A**

sede a dextris mé- is **B**

sede a dex- tris mé- is **C**

et to- tí- us ne- qui- tí-æ pur- gá- ta dis- cés- su **D**

quó-ni- am ad te Dómine áni- mam mé- am le- vá- vi **E**

et de- líctum me- um coram me est semper tibi so- li pec- cá- vi **F**

G

u **H**

I

tis **J**

de- li- ctó- rum me- ó- rum **K**

CR
JL

Dominant | Medial

Gló-ri-a in excélsis — Dé- o

Díxit Dóminus Dómino — mé- o

minus Dómino — mé- o

ra ab omni impugna- — tóris in- cúr- su

li-ca ánimam
est — sérvi confi- té-ri — tú- i Dómi-no

in-iqui- tá- tem mé- am — e-go a-
Patri et — gnósco Fí- li- o

stus ut palma flo- — ré- bit

non fú- e-rint do- mi- — ná-

et pro- té-ctor fá-ctus est mi- hi in sa-
ju- di- — lú- tem ci- um

Cadence   Intonation   Dominant

Et in ter- ra pax ho-mí- nibus bonæ vo-lun-

sede a   dextris

sede a   dex- tris

et to- ti- us ne- qui- ti-æ pur- gá- ta

quó-ni- am ad   te Dómine áni- mam mé- am

et de- lictum me- um coram me est semper tibi so- li

de- li- ctó- rum

www.ingramcontent.com/pod-product-compliance
Lightning Source LLC
Chambersburg PA
CBHW020753020726
47495CB00008B/2403

* 9 7 8 3 7 4 3 4 6 4 9 0 2 *